INTELLECTUAL AND PERSONALITY CHARACTERISTICS OF CHILDREN:
Social-Class and Ethnic-Group Differences

INTELLECTUAL AND PERSONALITY CHARACTERISTICS OF CHILDREN:
Social-Class and Ethnic-Group Differences

REGINA YANDO
Harvard University

VICTORIA SEITZ
EDWARD ZIGLER
Yale University

LAWRENCE ERLBAUM ASSOCIATES, PUBLISHERS
1979   Hillsdale, New Jersey

DISTRIBUTED BY THE HALSTED PRESS DIVISION OF
JOHN WILEY & SONS
New York   Toronto   London   Sydney

Lawrence Erlbaum Associates, Inc., Publishers
365 Broadway
Hillsdale, New Jersey 07642

Distributed solely by Halsted Press Division
John Wiley & Sons, Inc., New York

Library of Congress Cataloging in Publication Data

Yando, Regina.
  Intellectual and personality characteristics of
children.

  Bibliography: p.
  Includes indexes.
    1. Intellect.   2. Problem-solving.   3. Cognition
and culture.   4. Personality and culture.   5. Social
class—Psychological aspects.   6. Minorities—Psychology.
I. Seitz, Victoria, joint author.   II. Zigler, Edward
Frank, 1930–   joint author.   III. Title.
[DNLM: 1. Social class.   2. Ethnic groups.
3. Achievement—in infancy and childhood.   4. Child
behavior.   WS105.3 Y21i]
BF432.A1Y36   155.4'1   79-11503
ISBN 0-89859-001-9

Printed in the United States of America

Contents

1 Introduction

Social-class and ethnic-group membership have been found to be associated with a wide variety of personality, motivational, cognitive, and achievement behaviors in children in our society (see reviews by Deutsch, 1973; Deutsch, Katz, & Jensen, 1968; Dreger & Miller, 1960, 1968; Hess, 1970; Jencks et al., 1972; Loehlin, Lindzey, & Spuhler, 1975; Zigler & Child, 1973). The most consistent and frequently noted finding is that lower-class and minority group children generally perform less well than white middle-class children on standardized measures of intelligence and achievement.

A variety of explanations has been proposed to account for the consistency of this finding. Some investigators (Gottesman, 1965; Herrnstein, 1973; Jensen, 1970) have argued that social classes and/or racial groups represent populations with differing gene pools. Within such an interpretation, dissimilarities in behavior are viewed primarily as reflections of genetic group differences. A contrasting viewpoint is the sociocultural position that social-class and ethnic-group differences in behavior are the product of differences along a broad spectrum of experiential factors. Within this approach, investigators have disagreed as to the particular experiences that mediate the reported behavioral differences. Variations in childrearing practices have been emphasized by many theorists, with earlier studies focusing on personality differences and more recent studies on cognitive differences among social class and ethnic groups (see reviews by Caldwell, 1964; Deutsch, 1973; Hess & Shipman, 1967; Silverstein & Krate, 1975; Zigler & Child, 1973). Other researchers, working within a sociological and anthro-

1

pological framework, have emphasized differences in attitudes, values, and goals among social-class and ethnic groups. Still other investigators have stressed such diverse experiential factors as linguistic environment (Bernstein, 1961), biological environment (Pasamanick & Knobloch, 1961), and general environmental stimulation (Hunt, 1964). Situated between the extreme genetic and environmental positions is the interactionist view that social-class and ethnic-group differences in behavior reflect some not well specified combination of differences in both genetic predispositions and experiential histories. (See Loehlin et al., 1975, for a discussion of the controversy regarding the relative weight to be assigned to each of these variables in accounting for observed differences in performance.)

A careful reading of the literature on social-class (SES) and ethnic-group differences reveals that much research has been undertaken with the assumption that the behavior of white middle-class children represents the standard against which the behavior of all other children should be assessed. When a child's performance does not match this standard, the child is often considered "deficient," whether the "deficit" is viewed as the result of genetic differences or of a nonstimulating environment. A number of investigators (Baratz & Baratz, 1970; Cole & Bruner, 1971; Labov, 1970; Tulkin & Konner, 1973) have pointed out that research based upon this assumption has yielded a biased picture of the abilities in many groups of children in our society.

The authors believe that it is time for behavioral scientists to reject the deficit model and to adopt in its place a difference approach in which no group is considered to be inferior or superior to any other and in which differences among groups are viewed instead as important empirical phenomena to be investigated. A commitment to such a difference approach would urge behavioral scientists, and ultimately laymen, to deal with the central question of how human variation can be exploited for the enrichment of all members of society. With other thinkers of an evolutionary orientation (Dobzhansky, 1973; Loehlin et al., 1975), the authors are of the opinion that any objective analysis of human variation must result in the conclusion that variation should be welcomed rather than deplored. At the cultural level, many millenia of evolutionary selection make clear the survival value of human diversity. At the social level, employing a much more limited time frame, one can readily see how human diversity contributes to the richness of the social fabric. What is needed are the means to understand and share the contributions each social group can make to human life.

Within the difference orientation we are advocating, it is assumed that notions of superiority and inferiority can be replaced by the concept of human variation. Since every socioeconomic and ethnic group is adapting—whether for genetic or sociocultural reasons—to the ecological niche in which it exists, it would not be surprising to discover that various social-class and ethnic groups develop different profiles of behavior. A profile approach to human variation, though rare, can be found in the work of several investigators (Lesser, Fifer, & Clark, 1965; Loehlin et al., 1975; Stodolsky & Lesser, 1967).

A concept central to a difference orientation is the distinction between capacity and performance and the recognition that the absence of performance on a specific task does not necessarily imply the absence of the capacity thought to underlie the ability being measured. There is reason to believe, for example, that the "poor" performance of disadvantaged children often described in earlier studies may have resulted from the investigators' failure to devise optimal test environments. There is evidence that disadvantaged children are particularly apt to be affected by test anxiety and situational factors that lead them to perform less adequately on cognitive tests than their actual abilities would permit (Jacobson, Berger, Bergman, Millham, & Greeson, 1971; Seitz, Abelson, Levine, & Zigler, 1975; Thomas, Hertzig, Dryman, & Fernandez, 1971; Zigler, Abelson, & Seitz, 1973). Investigators involved in cross-cultural work have also found the capacity-performance distinction to be critical and have provided evidence that competent performance is most likely to be obtained from individuals only if the testing situations provide similarity to real problems in the individual's culture (Blurton Jones & Konner, 1976; Cole, Gay, Glick, & Sharp, 1971; Tyler, 1970).

The studies reported in this book were directed toward understanding how children from different social classes and ethnic groups behave in problem-solving situations. The difference model we have described provided the conceptual basis for these studies. It was therefore necessary to design the studies in a manner that would promote competent performance from different groups of children as well as permit a profile or pattern analysis of their behavior. Important considerations were the number and kinds of behavior to measure and the kinds of problem-solving tasks to use. Additionally, it was felt that the data would be strengthened if they were obtained from a variety of sources.

It seemed evident that the discovery of performance patterns would be facilitated if a large, rather than a small, number of behaviors were investigated. Single-variable research, while it is common in the social-class literature, readily lends itself to the characterization of groups as superior or inferior. The decision was therefore made to examine a wide range of behaviors. In general, our expectation was that the different groups of children would display different performance patterns but that no group would uniformly perform better than any other group if a wide variety of problems and behaviors were studied.

In considering the range of behaviors to be investigated, the decision was made to employ tasks that would tap motivation and personality characteristics rather than to focus on cognition alone. An inordinate amount of previous work has been concerned with social-class differences in formal cognition as measured by standard intelligence tests and school achievement measures. In contrast, personality, motivational, and emotional factors have been largely ignored, even though there is considerable agreement that such factors are important determinants of adaptation. As Zigler (1970, 1973) has noted, on every task with which a child is confronted, his or her performance is influenced simultaneously by three classes of variables: (1) formal cognitive abilities, such as memory and reasoning; (2) achievement factors, which involve knowledge about the content sampled by the task; and (3) motivational factors, which involve a wide variety of personality variables. (See Zigler & Butterfield, 1968, and Seitz et al., 1975, for a discussion of these three overlapping classes of variables.) The factors in the third category—motivational and personality factors—are most often implicated as being partially responsible for a child's poor school performance. As Holt (1964) and Stein (1971) have documented, a common description of the disadvantaged or minority group child by both educators and researchers is of a child who is not motivated to learn and who lacks the curiosity, persistence, and confidence necessary for problem-solving.

On the basis of suggestions found in the personality and motivation literature, we decided to investigate the children's performance in the following six areas: creativity, self-confidence, dependency, frustration threshold, curiosity, and autonomy. Measures were also obtained of children's self-concepts and their perception of how they were viewed by their teachers. Teachers, in turn, rated the children on the traits investigated. Additional data concerning school achievement was also collected.

The decision to obtain information from a variety of sources was based upon a strategy of converging operations (Garner, Hake, & Erikson, 1956). For example, if children from different groups can be distinguished on performance measures of self-confidence, do they also view themselves as more or less confident? Is there a relationship between such self-perception and the child's actual achievement level in school? If there is a group difference in a trait such as creativity, do other persons, especially the children's teachers, notice this difference? And what is the relationship between the children's beliefs about how their teachers see them and the ratings they receive from their teachers? By obtaining multiple measures from a variety of sources concerning the traits of interest, we hoped to achieve a more accurate and comprehensive interpretation of any behavioral differences discovered.

Because we wished to assess children's optimal performance, an effort was made to test the children under conditions which were as anxiety-free as possible. While all children were seen in a school setting, the testing situation was designed to suggest a game-like atmosphere. Children were told that they were evaluating games for a toy company and the investigator—a warm, sympathetic young woman—wanted to know how "kids their age" felt about the different games. Many of the tasks required physical activity on the part of the children, balancing objects and walking toy dogs through mazes for example. The children were also given prizes for their participation on some tasks, and encouragement and supportive feedback were provided frequently throughout the testing session. In short, every effort was made to create a situation that would be maximally enjoyable for the children, one which would allow them better to demonstrate their competencies.

To extend further the range of competence that the various groups of children might display, several types of problem-solving tasks were designed. One variable which was manipulated in the tasks given to the children was the number of correct solutions. Some tasks were designed to require a single solution. One task, for example, involved removing a token from a puzzle box; another was a jigsaw puzzle. Other tasks were designed to have multiple acceptable solutions or to have no solution at all. On several creativity tasks, for example, the child was called upon to generate a variety of responses. Additionally, on some tasks the children were confronted with insoluble problems in order to determine their threshold for frustration.

The solution variable was chosen in order to assess what Guilford (1956) has termed "convergent" and "divergent" thought processes. Guilford proposed that the thinking strategies required for problems with particular solutions differ from those required for problems which have no unique solution. The former are said to necessitate convergent thinking—a process of arriving at a solution that is fully specified by the nature of the information given (for example, solving an algebraic equation, or naming the author of the play "Hamlet"). Divergent thinking, in contrast, involves the search for and use of information that is only loosely related to what is provided in the problem situation. Given the problem, "Draw a house," for example, numerous acceptable solutions are possible. There are no unique solutions, neither are there absolute rules for choosing one solution in preference to another. Divergent thinking refers to the capacity to generate a complex and differentiated series of responses to a problem, and it has been most clearly associated with creative activity.

Previous studies have revealed that advantaged as compared to disadvantaged children perform better on tasks that require convergent thought strategies. Existing research on divergent thinking, however, has revealed no consistent differences between children from different social classes or races (Iscoe & Pierce-Jones, 1964; Rogers, 1968). These findings may be related to the fact that formal education stresses the development of convergent thinking (Bateson, 1972; Scribner & Cole, 1973; Torrance, 1965), and economically advantaged children as a group are generally more comfortable with academic demands. While schools provide a setting in which children may learn solutions to conventional problems, such as reading, spelling, and arithmetic, it is not as clear where children learn the skills of divergent thinking. It is not unlikely, however, that divergent thinking is fostered by experiences outside the school setting. In their everyday environments, children are constantly confronted with any number of problems which demand unconventional solutions. Further, disadvantaged compared with advantaged children may more often face such problems. When, for example, there is little money to purchase toys, an economically disadvantaged child may solve the problem by adapting an available item for play use. (This "necessity is the mother of invention" argument is not intended to be in praise of poverty but only as a recognition that some children may respond to economic privation by developing considerable strengths.) Consequently, while we were relatively confident in predicting social-class differences in performance on tasks that demanded convergent thinking, we more tentatively predicted either no differences or a difference favoring disadvantaged children on tasks demanding divergent, or creative, thinking skills.

Another variable manipulated in the problems given to the children was the verbal-performance dimension. Self-confidence, for example, was measured by tasks having a parallel structure, but requiring different skills (e.g., balancing in one task, reading in another). Creativity was measured by a number of tasks, some of which required verbal and some of which required physical responses. In general we expected that social-class differences might be greater on verbal tasks (which tend to be correlated with general cognitive test performance) than on nonverbal tasks.

In addition to studying children's behavior, we interviewed the children in order to assess their self-concept. Previous researchers have generally found that children from minority and/or lower socio-economic-status groups in this society are likely to have lower self-esteem than are white and/or higher socioeconomic-status group children (Deutsch et al., 1968; Kardiner & Ovesey, 1951; Nobles, 1973; Pettigrew, 1964; Rosenberg & Simmons, 1971; Soares & Soares, 1969; Trowbridge, 1972). In the present investigation, it seemed reasonable to expect a replication of these findings. However, ethnic-group and social-class variables were separated in the present investigation. Since most previous research has failed to separate these variables, no specific predictions regarding ethnic-group differences were made. There is some evidence from studies with adults that a disparity can exist between a person's perceived self and how that person believes he or she is viewed by others (Achenbach & Zigler, 1963; Brownfain, 1952). We considered that it would be of interest, therefore, to investigate both the "real" and the "social self" perceptions of the children. Specifically, the children were asked both about their own self-perceptions and about their perceptions of how their teachers viewed them.

In addition to the data obtained directly from the children, the children's teachers were asked to rate them on the same traits under investigation (i.e., creativity, self-confidence, etc.) as well as on class-room achievement and other variables. For most children, the results of standardized academic achievement tests were also available. Accordingly, the relationships among the teachers' ratings of children, the children's perceptions of how they were rated, their self-perceptions, and their actual school performance could be ascertained. This information was of particular interest given the argument of several investigators that the expectation of failure by disadvantaged children and their teachers may underlie these children's generally poorer performance in school (McDermott & Aron, 1978; Rist, 1973; Rosenthal & Jacobson, 1968). On the standardized achievement tests, it was expected that advantaged children would perform better than disadvantaged children except in those groups that were equated on IQ and mental age.

Because the studies reported in this book were primarily exploratory, few specific predictions were made beyond those just described and the general expectation that children from the two SES groups would show different performance patterns across different tasks. No predictions were made regarding the performance of different ethnic groups. The literature is simply too sparse to warrant making predictions, given the fact that most prior studies of ethnic-group differences in behavior have been contaminated with social-class effects.

Finally, the question of what constitutes the optimal design of studies that investigate social-classes and ethnic-group differences in behavior was considered. The most frequently employed design equates children of different social class on chronological age (CA) alone and then attributes any differences in behavior which are discovered to social-class membership. However, interpretations of the differences found in such studies are made difficult by the fact that such groups of children may be at different developmental levels (Zigler & Child, 1973). The differences found in behavior could therefore be just as readily attributed to differences in average developmental level as to social-class membership per se. One could control for the developmental-level variable by matching groups of lower- and middle-class children on IQ, mental age (MA), and chronological age. Unfortunately, such a matched groups design would result in the comparison of nonrepresentative samples. That is, given the IQ distribution usually found in the different social-class populations, a matched groups design would involve a comparison of middle-class children who are somewhat lower in IQ than are most middle-class children, with lower-class children who have relatively higher IQs than most lower-class children.

Confronted with the dilemma of selecting between two designs, both of which are flawed, the authors made the decision to conduct two studies: one matching social-class and ethnic groups on MA and IQ, and one in which the groups were equated only on chronological age. Although this decision was suggested in Meehl's (1970, 1971) analyses of the methodological issues involved, we could find no other instance in the literature where investigators employed such a combined design approach. It was our hope that such a dual approach would result not only in findings that could be interpreted with confidence, but also in the clarification of methodological and design issues present in research directed at the investigation of behavioral differences associated with social-class and ethnic-group membership.

OVERVIEW OF THE INVESTIGATION

Two separate studies were conducted in the present investigation. In the first study, economically advantaged second- and third-grade children were compared with economically disadvantaged children who were equivalent in IQ, chronological age, and, therefore, also in mental age. In addition, all children were from two-parent homes and none had failed a grade in school. Relatively stringent criteria were employed to define socioeconomic status in order to produce two nonoverlapping groups (see Chapter 2). Within each SES group, half of the children were black, half were white, and the sexes were equally represented.

The children were compared on an extensive battery of performance measures designed to tap creativity, frustration threshold, self-confidence, curiosity, autonomy, and dependency. Interviews were obtained with the children in order to gain information about their self-concepts and their perceptions of how their teachers viewed them. Teachers were asked to rate each child on the attributes being investigated and on the child's classroom achievement. In addition to the performance, interview, and ratings data, standardized achievement test scores and family size information were obtained for most children. Data on the racial composition of the child's school and whether or not the child was bused to school were also recorded. The first study will be referred as the "matched groups" study.

In the second study, which will be referred as the "typical groups" study, economically advantaged and economically disadvantaged children were defined in the same manner as in the first study. The second study involved children who were of the same age as those in the matched groups study (8-year-olds). Sample selection, however, was random with regard to IQ and MA, and the children were therefore presumed to be representative of the social-class groups delineated in the matched groups study. As before, half of the children within each SES group were black, half were white, and the sexes were equally represented. Unlike the earlier study, family composition and school retention were ignored in selection so that these variables varied freely in the samples in approximation of their true population values. Data collection was identical to that in the matched groups study.

Two subsidiary issues were examined in both studies. Variation in presence or absence of the father in the home was found to be extensive among the disadvantaged children in the typical groups study, and variation in the racial composition of the schools was substantial for disadvantaged black children in both studies. Accordingly, comparisons were made of: (1) disadvantaged children from two-parent with those from single-parent families; and (2) disadvantaged black children who attended predominantly black schools with those who attended predominantly white schools. In order to make possible comparisons of the matched and typical studies on the father's presence or absence issue, a father-absent sample of disadvantaged children was added to the investigation. This sample was comparable to the disadvantaged children in the matched groups study in every respect except that the children came from single-parent homes. Advantaged children in the typical groups study were found to be almost entirely from two-parent families; this variable was therefore not explored for the advantaged children in the present investigation.

The remainder of the book is organized as follows. Chapter 2 describes the method employed in conducting the studies, including how subjects were selected and how tasks were designed, administered, and scored. Chapter 3 presents the statistical results of the studies. In Chapter 4, we discuss the findings and their implications.

2 Method

DEFINITION OF CRITERIA EMPLOYED
IN ESTABLISHING SUBJECT GROUPS

Socioeconomic Rating

Three indices were employed in the determination of socioeconomic standing: occupation, education, and residence. In order to be assigned to either the advantaged or disadvantaged groups, criteria for all three indices had to be met. Data regarding parental occupation and education were obtained from school officials; confidentiality of information was maintained by means of a coding system.

Occupation. The occupation of the head of the household was rated according to the 7-point Hollingshead and Redlich Scale (1958). According to this scale, ranks 1, 2, and 3 are defined as including executives, proprietors, professionals, and high-level administrative personnel; whereas ranks 6 and 7 include only semiskilled and unskilled workers. In order to minimize overlap and sharpen socioeconomic differences, only those children whose parents ranked in the extreme groups were employed in the studies. An advantaged grouping was assigned to ranks 1, 2, and 3, and a disadvantaged grouping was assigned to ranks 6 and 7. Unemployed heads of households qualified for disadvantaged assignment only if they were potentially within ranks 6 and 7. The eliminated ranks included owners of small nonindependent businesses, clerical and sales workers, technicians, and skilled workers.

The distribution of parental occupational status for the selected sample is illustrated in Table 2.1.

In the typical groups study, 27 of the 40 disadvantaged black and 29 of the 40 disadvantaged white children were from working poor families. The remaining 24 families could be considered nonworking poor. In the matched groups study, all of the disadvantaged white father-present (N = 24) and all but one of the disadvantaged black father-present (N = 23) sample were working poor. However, both the black and white disadvantaged father-absent groups were considered nonworking poor, since no mothers were employed.

TABLE 2.1

Distribution of Sample According to SES Assignment and Position
on the Hollingshead Scale

Hollingshead Scale Level	Group			
	Advantaged		Disadvantaged	
	Black	White	Black	White
Matched Groups Study[a]				
1	14	20		
2	8	4		
3	2	0		
4				
5				
6			16	15
7			7	9
(7a)[b]			1	0
Typical Groups Study				
1	20	25		
2	19	12		
3	1	3		
4				
5				
6			16	15
7			11	14
(7a)			13	11

[a]An additional sample of 48 disadvantaged children from father-absent homes is not represented in this table; all 48 of these chidlren were from level 7a homes.

[b]The number, 7a, designates a group that is unemployed and with no known skill.

Education.   A simple two-group distinction, college or no college, was employed for the purpose of rating a parent's educational attainment. All children who were grouped as disadvantaged had parents who had not attended school beyond high school. Children in the advantaged group had at least one parent with two or more years of college training.

Residence.   Children in the disadvantaged group were from families whose dwellings were either in housing projects or in residences which were within poverty districts. Approximately 78% of the families resided in housing projects. For a family to qualify for housing, the income level had to be below $7900 for a family of four. All children in the advantaged group resided in areas characterized by individual dwellings ranging in value upward from approximately $40,000 in 1971.

Ethnicity

The sample was limited to children whose parents were born in this country and were of the same broadly defined ethnic group as the child. Children were selected for grouping as "black" (restricted to "Afro-Americans") or "white" strictly by the identification accorded to them by their community. Numerous social and educational policy decisions are based on the social criterion of racial assignment. Since the concerns of this study are related to such policy decisions, the use of the social criterion is most appropriate.

Father's Presence or Absence

Data concerning the father's presence or absence from the home were obtained from teachers and principals. These groupings, then, are based strictly upon the educational community's perception of the father's presence in the family.

IQ and MA Scores

IQ information was acquired from the school authorities. If an IQ score was unavailable for a child, it was obtained from the Peabody Picture

Vocabulary Test Form B, administered by a trained examiner prior to experimental testing. Although most schools routinely administer group IQ tests, they frequently vary in the choice of test used. For both studies, five different but fairly comparable group IQ tests were represented. These were: Otis-Lennon Mental Abilities Test, Science Research Associates Short Test of Educational Ability, Kuhlmann-Anderson Intelligence Test, California Test of Mental Maturity, and Lorge-Thorndike Intelligence Test. All five of these tests employ a deviation IQ, and all have means of 100 and standard deviations of 16.

SELECTION OF SUBJECTS

Matched Groups Study

The basic sample for the matched groups study consisted of a total of 96 children, 48 economically advantaged and 48 economically disadvantaged. Each economic group consisted of an equal number of white and black children, of which half were girls and half were boys. All children were from families in which both parents were present in the home. In order to investigate the effects of father presence versus absence, another group of 48 economically disadvantaged children from father-absent households was added to the sample. As in the primary sample, male and female black and white children were equally represented. The following comments refer to all 144 children.

Children were drawn from the second and third grades of 36 schools in several urban areas of Massachusetts. No child showed evidence of gross physical or emotional disturbances. Children who had failed a grade in school or who had an IQ below 85 were excluded. Subjects were matched on both CA and MA. The mean CA, MA, and IQ scores for each group are presented in Table 2.2.

No attempt was made to control for the religious background of the children. Based on minimal information (enrollment in parochial schools and, if available, school records), it was estimated that approximately 50% of this sample was Catholic. Although no gross difference was found between economic groups, within the advantaged sample the majority of blacks were not Catholic whereas the majority of whites were. Also, most of the children, both black and white, from father-absent homes were non-Catholic.

TABLE 2.2
Mean CA, MA, and IQ Scores for Each Group of Children in the Matched Groups Study

Group	N	CA (in yrs.)		MA (in yrs.)		IQ	
		$\bar{X}$	SD	$\bar{X}$	SD	$\bar{X}$	SD
Advantaged black							
Females	12	8.3	.5	8.8	.9	103.3	5.5
Males	12	8.4	.8	8.8	.6	104.6	7.7
Total	24	8.4	.7	8.8	.8	104.0	7.0
Advantaged white							
Females	12	8.4	.5	8.6	.9	100.1	7.9
Males	12	8.6	.3	8.8	.9	100.4	7.3
Total	24	8.5	.4	8.7	.9	100.2	7.9
Disadvantaged black (father present)							
Females	12	8.4	.8	8.6	.9	99.7	6.3
Males	12	8.6	.6	8.7	.4	99.0	7.9
Total	24	8.5	.7	8.6	.8	99.3	7.4
Disadvantaged white (father present)							
Females	12	8.6	.7	8.7	1.1	99.5	7.0
Males	12	8.6	.5	8.6	.8	99.5	7.9
Total	24	8.6	.6	8.7	1.0	99.5	7.8
Disadvantaged black (father absent)							
Females	12	8.7	.6	9.0	.8	101.2	7.1
Males	12	8.5	.3	8.6	.8	98.9	7.7
Total	24	8.6	.5	8.8	.8	100.1	7.7
Disadvantaged white (father absent)							
Females	12	8.4	.8	8.4	1.2	98.5	8.6
Males	12	8.4	.7	8.7	.8	100.8	5.7
Total	24	8.4	.8	8.6	1.1	99.6	7.6

Typical Groups Study

A total of 160 children, 80 economically advantaged and 80 economically disadvantaged, served as subjects for the typical groups study. Each group consisted of an equal number of black and white children, of which half were girls and half were boys. Groups were matched by CA only. While no child in the sample showed evidence of gross intellectual, physical, or emotional problems, children were not excluded for having failed a school grade or for having an IQ below 85, as in the matched groups study. The mean CA, MA, and IQ scores for each group are presented in Table 2.3.

The sample was drawn from the second and third grades of 29 schools in several urban areas of Massachusettes (11 of these schools had also contributed subjects to the matched groups study). In terms of religious background, the minimal information available indicated that approximately 25% of the sample was Catholic. No gross differences were found between social classes or ethnic groups in representation of religious affiliation.

TABLE 2.3

Mean CA, MA, and IQ Scores for Each Group of Children in the Typical Groups Study

Group	N	CA (in yrs.) $\bar{X}$	SD	MA (in yrs.) $\bar{X}$	SD	IQ $\bar{X}$	SD
Advantaged black							
Females	20	8.2	.7	8.6	1.2	102.0	12.0
Males	20	8.3	.8	8.7	1.0	104.0	12.4
Total	40	8.3	.8	8.6	1.1	103.0	12.4
Advantaged white							
Females	20	8.1	.6	9.2	1.0	112.2	10.1
Males	20	8.2	.6	9.8	1.0	117.9	12.3
Total	40	8.2	.6	9.5	1.0	115.0	11.4
Disadvantaged black							
Females	20	8.3	.8	7.6	.8	90.3	10.1
Males	20	8.6	.7	8.2	.9	92.8	9.6
Total	40	8.5	.8	7.9	.9	91.6	10.0
Disadvantaged white							
Females	20	8.2	.7	8.7	1.2	102.8	7.7
Males	20	8.4	.8	8.9	.8	105.3	8.8
Total	40	8.3	.8	8.8	1.0	104.1	8.4

GENERAL PROCEDURE

A young white[1] female with teaching experience served as examiner for both studies. All children were seen individually in one approximately 1½-hour-long session, which was interrupted midway with a rest break.

The examiner met the child at his or her classroom and introduced herself as a person who worked for a game company. She explained to the child that the company she worked for had just manufactured some new toys for children his or her age. The company was interested in knowing whether or not children would like them, and she was wondering if he or she would play the games and give his or her opinion. All children were told that they need participate only if they wanted; no child selected for the study refused. The intent of the introduction and further instructions given to the child was to aid him or her in approaching the testing session as a nonacademically related situation. Assuming that some children might be adversely affected by test anxiety, such instructions seemed particularly necessary to encourage the child to perform at his or her best, given the school setting.

The examiner took the child to the testing room and administered the tasks, which are described in the next section of this chapter, in the following order: (a) Find-the-Surprise—Trial 1; (b) Self-Concept Inventory; (c) Unusual Uses; (d) Balancing Game; (e) Opening Doors; (f) Dog and Bone; (g) Find-the-Surprise—Trial 2; (h) Perception of Teacher's View Interview; (i) Walk-the-Board; (j) Product Improvement; (k) Reading Game; (l) Find-the-Surprise—Trial 3; (m) Token-in-the-Box; (n) Puzzle; (o) Find-the-Surprise—Trial 4; (p) Five-Objects. This order was chosen to provide frequent shifts between physical and verbal activities in order to keep the long session from becoming tedious for the children. The majority of the tasks were administered while the examiner and the child were seated at a table. At the end of the session, children were asked which of the games had been their favorite and which they had liked the least.

Considerable attention was devoted to ensuring that each child left the testing session with some sense of accomplishment and without a

---

[1]The authors recognize that there is contradictory literature on experimenter effects when children are tested by examiners of different races (see Sattler, 1970). Until the effects of race of experimenter on children's performance are clearly understood, it is necessary to investigate this variable fully when it is introduced. This would require multiple experimenters of each race (as in Yando, Zigler, & Gates, 1971), and in the present investigation it would have required a substantial increase in sample size. We therefore used only one experimenter.

feeling that he or she had failed or done poorly. Although many of the tasks were potentially frustrating, they were carefully designed to be no more anxiety-provoking than those problem-solving situations that a child would normally encounter in his or her everyday environment. After frustration-type tasks, examiner statements were made to reduce any feelings of failure that the child might have incurred. A child would be told, for example, that a game was "not a good one for kids your age," or that "this game should be sent back to the company, it's no fun." In addition, positive reinforcement was offered for the manner in which the child played. Each child left the test situation with at least four toys as evidence of his or her competence and successful performance. No child was forced to participate in any task, particularly the Walk-the-Board game, which he or she found anxiety-provoking. Perhaps the best evidence regarding the positive emotional ambiance of the test situation was the fact that no child refused to play any of the games or asked to leave the testing situation; further, most children asked to remain even after the session had been completed.

CHILDREN'S PERFORMANCE MEASURES

The selection and construction of tasks for this investigation were guided by several principles. The first of these was our belief in the desirability of employing behavioral rather than paper-and-pencil tasks. Given the limitation of much previous research to measures demanding a high level of reading ability and conventional academic skills, the present tasks, with the exception of one (the Reading Game), were constructed to minimize academic achievement. A related consideration was the elimination of a test-like appearance of the tasks. Under the assumption that text anxiety has a particularly adverse effect on the performance of children from disadvantaged populations, the tasks were made to be as game-like as possible. An attempt was also made to employ tasks that would elicit both verbal and physical responses from the children (e.g., to tap both verbal and nonverbal creativity). Finally, an effort was made to adapt existent tasks, which have been used with children, rather than to develop entirely new tasks.

In total, 14 tasks yielding 26 measures were employed. These were ordered within six face-valid construct areas: creativity, self-confidence, autonomy, curiosity, frustration threshold, and dependency. The constructs investigated and the experimental tasks and measures used are summarized in Table 2.4. Task descriptions and measure-

TABLE 2.4
Task and Performance Measures Used to Investigate the Constructs Under
Study

Construct	Task	Measure
Creativity	Verbal creativity tasks	Originality per response
		Highest originality
		Total fluency
		Total flexibility
	Dog and Bone	Quality per path
		Highest quality path
	Token-in-the-Box	Quality per attempt
		Highest quality attempt
	Five-Objects	Highest number of objects used in most complex solution
Self-confidence	Reading Task	First level attempted
		Mean level attempted
		Risk score
	Balancing Task	First level attempted
		Mean level attempted
		Risk score
	Token-in-the-Box	Confidence in ability to succeed
Autonomy	Find-the-surprise	First choice
		Total number of autonomous responses
Curiosity	Opening Doors	Number of blank doors
Frustration threshold	Dog and Bone	Time to frustration statement
	Token-in-the-Box	Number of attempts
	Puzzle	Total length of time
Dependency	Walk-the-Board	Number of handholding requests
	Puzzle	Number of dependency statements per second
	Five-Objects	Number of requests for feedback
		Need for prompting

ments, ordered within construct areas, are presented next. The full description of each task is provided under the construct for which it was primarily designed. Mention of all relevant tasks is made for each construct.

Creativity Measures

Five tasks were employed to measure divergent thinking. Performance on two of the tasks, Unusual Uses and Product Improvement, was dependent on a child's verbal production (described below as the "verbal creativity tasks"). The remaining three tasks, Token-in-the-Box, Dog and Bone, and Five-Objects, were nonverbal measures of creativity.

Verbal Creativity Tasks.   There is a substantial research literature concerned with measuring verbal creativity. In the present study we relied upon two tasks which have been used with adults by Guilford and his associates (Guilford, Wilson, Christensen, & Lewis, 1951) and with children by Torrance and his associates (Torrance, 1965; Yamamoto & Chimbidis, 1966). Slight modifications of the tasks were introduced in order to employ objects which were certain to be familiar to all of the children in the sample. Also, the tasks were presented as evaluation-free games. Several studies (Wallach & Kogan, 1965; Ward, 1968) have found that a more clear differentiation between creativity and general intelligence can be achieved if the measurement of creativity is done within an evaluation-free context.

In the first of these tasks, "Unusual Uses" (Guilford et al., 1951), a teaspoon was employed. The examiner placed the spoon on the table in front of the child and said: "I bet you get pretty sick of using spoons every single day for the same old thing, like eating, right? Well, just for fun, let's pretend you could use spoons for *anything* at all. Try really hard to think of things that nobody else would think of to do with a spoon, OK? Now, tell me lots of really neat things you can do with a spoon."

The child was given 3 minutes for the task, although he or she was unaware that there was a time limit or that he or she was being timed. All responses were recorded, and positive verbal reinforcement was given after each response. Prompting statements, such as "I bet if you tried *real* hard you could think of something," were used if the child wanted to stop before the end of the 3 minutes.

The second task, "Product Improvement" (Guilford et al., 1951), employed an ordinary, unlabeled tin can. The examiner placed the tin can on the table in front of the child and presented the task as follows:

> You know, the game company I work for tries very hard to make the kinds of games kids will really like. One of the things we're working on is how to make something really far out from a tin can, but we need your help. How about telling me as many ways as you can to change the tin can, to make it different, so it's a fun thing to play with, OK? Tell me as many ways as you can think of to *change* it.

As in the Unusual Uses task, the child was given a 3-minute time limit, positive reinforcement after every response, and prompting if needed.

The creativity scoring system was adapted from procedures which are described in detail by Yamamoto (1964). Three basic measures, "fluency," "flexibility," and "originality," were obtained on each task. Fluency was determined simply by the raw number of acceptable answers the child produced. Bizarre, repetitious, and irrelevant responses were considered unacceptable and not counted. The flexibility score was based upon the number of different categories of usage suggested by the child. For example, a tin can may be used as a container, but it may also be used as a decoration, as a weighting device on a pendulum, as a source of aluminum, and as part of a makeshift walkie-talkie. The child who suggested that a tin can could be changed into a pencil holder, into a planter, and into a container for paper clips was given a score of 3 for fluency of output, but a score of 1 for flexibility since all of the suggested uses are within the single category of serving as a container. A stringent flexibility scoring procedure was employed, crediting any given category only once (Torrance, 1965). This procedure differs somewhat from the Yamamoto (1964) system in that it does not give credit for the return to a previous idea. The Yamamoto system is analogous to conceptualizing the creative thinking effort as a perceptual figure–ground task in which the percept shifts from one state to another, and flexibility is a measure of the frequency of shifting. The Torrance procedure, on the other hand, is more concerned with identifying the number of different conceptual shifts the child is able to make. In all, 39 categories similar to those employed by Torrance, 22 for the Unusual Uses task and 17 for the Product Improvement task, were derived from the data. For scoring, two judges independently assigned the responses to the established categories. A Pearson Product-Moment correlation of .85 was obtained for the category assignment of acceptable responses from the Product Improvement task. The overall percentage for agreement concerning response assignment into categories for the Unusual Uses task was 93%.

The originality scoring procedure was a combination of the normative approach (Torrance and Yamamoto), which judges an original response relative to the responses produced by the subject sample, and the subjective ratings approach (Guilford), which judges a response relative to a presumed absolute standard of originality. The procedure was as follows. In order to score for originality, two aspects of a response were considered: (1) the category to which it belonged; and (2) its distinctiveness relative to other responses in the same category. First, two judges rank ordered the 39 "flexibility" categories from least to most creative. Since many of the categories were of similar creative expression, the rank-ordered list was divided into seven groups, each of which was then assigned scores of 0, for the least creative, to 3, for the most creative (with increments of ½ point for each of the seven ascending groups). Spearman Rank Order correlations for interjudge reliability were .91 for the Unusual Uses task, and .83 for the Product Improvement task. Second, independent of the category ranking but within each of the groups, all responses relative to each other were scored on a 3-point scale from least to most unusual. For this procedure, Pearson Product-Moment correlations of .86 and .81 were obtained for the two judges' scoring of the Unusual Uses and Product Improvement tasks, respectively. The originality score was the sum of the category and the individual response scores. For computational purposes, the child's originality score was divided by his or her fluency score in order to produce an originality per response index, since pilot work with these tasks had shown that the fluency and originality scores were highly correlated. In addition, the highest originality score ever produced by the child (maximum = 6) was employed to provide a kind of absolute capacity gauge of the child's ability to produce original responses, regardless of whether she or he was consistent in producing high-level responses.

Results from the pilot data revealed that the Unusual Uses and Product Improvement tasks were highly correlated, a finding also replicated in the full study. These tasks were considered to be replications of each other which provided the child with two separate occasions to demonstrate his or her verbal creativity. Scores were therefore averaged across the two tasks, and the four dependent variables employed in all analyses were: (1) fluency; (2) flexibility; (3)

originality per response; and (4) the highest originality response produced.

Token-in-the-Box Game.   In this game, the type and number of strategies a child used in attempting to remove a token from a small box which had a number of differently shaped cutout slots were considered to be measures of the child's creative abilities. The materials for the task consisted of a yellow plastic token, 3.8 cm in diameter and .3 cm thick, an unpainted plywood box, 21.6 cm × 15.2 cm × 10.2 cm, and an unsharpened pencil. In the top of the box was a slot just large enough for the token to pass through. The box also contained nine additional openings: three in each side, one in each end, and another in the top. The openings, which appeared large enough for the token to pass through, were of different geometric (e.g., trapezoid, oval) and free-form shapes. However, only one opening, the slot in the top of the box, was more than 3.5 cm at its widest point. That opening, therefore, was the only opening through which the token could pass. The task was presented as follows:

You've really been doing well today, (child's name), and since you're such a good game player, I'm going to tell you about another game that not all the boys and girls get to play—you see, it's a pretty special game. Now, here's a box. [The examiner held the box in her hand during the explanation]. See, it has holes cut out on the top and sides, and they're all different shapes. I'm going to put this plastic chip [held up chip] into the box, and what you have to do is get it out. You can use this to help you if you want [placed pencil on the table]. Now, before you play, you have to tell me whether or not you think you can get the chip out. Do you think you can? [The child was given time to answer yes or no. If no, the examiner said, "Well you'd really be helping us a lot if you just tried it, OK?," then continued with the instructions.] Fine. Now, one other thing: You can stop any time you feel you want to, but you'll have to *tell* me when you want to stop, OK?

The examiner then put the token into the box through the slot, placed the box in the child's hands, and started timing, keeping the watch out of the child's sight. The task ended only when 5 minutes were up or when the child said, "I want to stop," "I give up," etc. When 5 minutes had elapsed, the examiner stopped the child by saying: "Gee, we have so many other games to play, maybe we'd better stop now. [The examiner took the box and continued with the instructions.] We were a little worried that the game might be too hard for kids your age, and if *you* can't do it, I guess we'd better send it back to the company."

The scoring system was derived in the following manner. First, an attempt was defined as a marked change in the pattern of a child's activity to remove the token from the box. For example, if the child had been trying to remove the token from one opening and switched to another opening, this would have been recorded as a change from one attempt to another. After extensive pilot testing, it was decided that during testing the examiner would record four types of information for each attempt: (1) the position of the box (on the table, off the table); (2) handling of the box (shaking, purposeful shaking, or tipping); (3) how many and which type of openings were employed in attempting to remove the token; and (4) instruments (fingers, pencil) employed. Upon completion of data collection for the studies, all protocols were examined in order to determine the strategies that children employed to remove the token. The following eight strategies, presented in an ascending order of effectiveness, were identified:

1. *Random shaking* of the box (½ point).
2. *Tipping* the box so that the token was over one of the openings and then *shaking* the box to remove it (1 point).
3. With the box *on the table*, employing an *instrument* to remove the token through the *same opening* into which the instrument was inserted (2 points).
4. With the box *on the table*, employing *one or more instruments* to remove the token through *an opening other than* the one through which *one* of the instruments was inserted (3 points).
5. With the box *off the table*, employing the *finger* to remove the token from the *same opening* into which the finger was inserted (4 points).
6. With the box *off the table*, employing the *pencil* to remove the token from the *same opening* into which the pencil was inserted (5 points).
7. With the box *off the table*, employing *two instruments* to remove the token through the *same opening* into which one of the instruments was inserted (6 points).
8. With the box *off the table*, inserting the *pencil* into *one opening* in order to remove the token from *another opening* (7 points).

The "quality" score for each of the child's attempts to remove the token, then, was derived from this category scale. The measure used for analysis was the child's total quality score divided by the number of attempts, a score which provides a quality-per-response measure intended to be analogous to the originality-per-response measure on the verbal creativity tasks. The highest quality response ever produced by the child was also recorded.

In addition to tapping the child's creativity, the Token-in-the-Box was also intended to provide one self-confidence measure and one measure of the child's frustration threshold. The task and these measures are described in the discussion of those respective constructs.

Dog and Bone Game.   In seeking another performance analogue to the verbal creativity measures, a modification of a task developed by Banta (1967) was employed. Unlike tasks requesting the child to verbally generate many alternative solutions to a problem, the Banta task requires the child to physically act out the solutions. Pilot work suggested that in addition to generating creativity information, the Dog and Bone task, like the Token-in-the-Box, might also provide information about frustration thresholds.

The materials consisted of: four trees made of construction paper and mounted on separate 22.9 cm × 24.1 cm pieces of blue plywood; a stuffed dog, 16.5 cm tall; and a plastic bone, 10.2 cm in length. The examiner placed the four trees on the floor in two rows of two each. The stuffed dog was positioned in front of the assembled materials, the bone to the rear. The examiner sat on the floor with the child to her right and introduced the task by saying:

> Here's another game for you. Here is a dog, and here is the dog's bone. The dog is hungry and wants his bone. One way he can get to it is to come up this way [the examiner demonstrated a straight path]. Another way he can go is around this way [demonstrated going to the left of the tree in the bottom left-hand corner, then in to the center of the trees and straight up to the bone]. Now, you take the dog and find another way for him to get to his bone.

On Trial 2 and the remaining trials the examiner said, "Now find another way for him to get to his bone," or "How about another way?" If the child said he or she could not think of any more, he or she was encouraged with statements such as "Try real hard" or "I bet you can do it." The task was terminated after two statements of encouragment had to be given for one trial and 35 seconds that elapsed with no attempt being made, or after the 12th trial.

The number of trials that the child completed was recorded, as was the nature of each path she or he produced. Creativity was scored using Banta's system (1967). (A 2-month test–retest coefficient of .82 and an internal consistency coefficient of .94 were reported by Banta.) Each trial was assigned 0, 1, 2, or 3 points, depending on the complexity of the path. Only innovative, nonrepeated paths were scored. In order to derive a creativity measure which would be independent of the child's persistence, the total complexity score (ranging from 0 to 36 points) was divided by the number of paths completed (maximum = 12 paths) to generate an average creative quality per path score. The highest complexity score that the child had earned for any path was also recorded. As a measure of threshold for frustration, the time had elapsed until the child made a first indication of frustration and wishing to stop (e.g., "I can't think of anything else") was also noted.

In addition to the various verbal and nonverbal creativity measures described, one measure from the "Five-Objects" game—the highest number of objects used by the child to create a solution—was employed. Since the Five-Objects game was designed primarily as a measure of dependency, it will be described in a later section.

Self-Confidence Measures

The child's answer (yes or no) to the question of whether or not he or she expected to be successful on the Token-in-the-Box game described above was used as one self-confidence measure. The following tasks were also designed to provide such information.

Balancing Game. In the Balancing game, the child was given repeated opportunities to choose the level of difficulty at which he or she wished to perform the task. It was assumed that the child's preference to engage in an easy as compared to a challenging task is related to the child's confidence in his or her abilities. In order to inspire all children to complete the task, a reward was offered for successful completion in the form of a certificate that would be seen by teacher and principal. The game was deliberately constructed to represent a nonacademic type of skill in order to explore whether or not some children, particularly the disadvantaged, might more readily display confidence (risk-taking) on this task as opposed to a more academically structured task (the Reading task, described below).

Three large paper bags labeled "easy," "a little hard," and "very hard," each containing nine boxes of different sizes and colors, were employed for this task. Each box contained groups of items to be balanced that corresponded to the levels of difficulty on each label. The balancing level of difficulty was determined by pilot testing. Examples of "easy" items were: three small flat stones; three plastic refrigerator-dish covers; three small pads of paper. In three of the boxes marked "a little hard" were: 12 unsharpened pencils; 10 marbles; and six small balls of aluminum foil. Items in the "very hard" category included: four empty frozen juice cans; 10 large wooden beads; and five empty metal adhesive-tape rolls. The top box in each bag was labeled "sample," and its contents were shown to the child as an example of the level of difficulty of the items in that bag.

The three bags were lined up on the floor in order of difficulty, with the "easy" bag to the left of the child. Parallel to the bags was a 1.82 m strip of 1.9 cm colored tape along which the child was to walk while balancing the items. To the right of the bags were a small covered dish containing about 30 yellow plastic tokens, a covered box of assorted small toys, a metal stand holding a certificate that the child could win, and a score card explaining the rules for winning the certificate and toys.

The game began with both the child and the examiner seated at the table. The examiner gave the following instructions:

You know, my company's interested in sports, too, and we've made a new sports game we'd like you to try. It's a balancing game. Come on over here. [Examiner and child moved to floor in front of bags.] See these bags? Each of them has boxes in it, and inside each box are things for you to balance, to carry on one hand. What you'll do in this game is balance things and walk along this tape [pointed] at the same time. Come on over here and let me show you what you'll have to do [led child to end of tape]. I'll use these [held up two tokens]. Watch me, and I'll show you and tell you the rules at the same time. [Demonstrated.] Stand in front of the tape. Make your hand flat like this [palm flat, fingers straight, thumb along side of palm] and *keep* it that way. Pile your things on it like this [placed tokens on palm]. Stretch out your arm and keep it stretched out as you walk along the tape. At this end turn, keeping one foot on the tape, and walk back, keeping your hand and arm stretched out flat. [End of demonstration, led child back to bags.] This bag has things in it that are easy to balance, see? [Opened sample box, showed contents to the child.] This bag has things in it that are a little harder [showed sample]. And this bag has very hard things [showed sample]. [Sample boxes were not returned to bags.] Now, you'll have six turns to pick things to balance from any of these bags. If you walk the tape forward and back four times without dropping anything, you will win a special certificate that your

teacher and your principal will see. Here it is. [Read certificate.] "This is
to certify that (child's name) is a Grand Prize Winner in the I & S Game
Company's annual balancing contest." Now, you'll be able to win prizes
in this game, too. Each time you walk along the tape with things from the
easy bag, without dropping anything, I'll give you one of these tokens
[pointed]. I'll give you three tokens when you balance things from the
little hard bag, and you'll get five tokens if you balance things from the
very hard bag without dropping anything. You can buy any of these toys
(pointed) with your tokens. Each toy costs five tokens, so the more tokens
you have, the more toys you can get, OK? Let's use this score card so it
will be easier to remember [showed card to child]. See, you have six turns.
Every time you balance the things from a box without dropping anything,
I'll put a check mark here. If you balance things four times from any bag
without dropping anything, you get the certificate. But the number of
tokens and toys you get depends on the bag you choose. OK? Pick a box.

The child then picked any box from any bag. The examiner carried
the box to the end of the tape and held it while the child stacked the
items on his or her palm. The child started walking as soon as he or she
was ready. When the child began to walk, he or she was reminded, if
necessary, to keep his or her palm flat and his or her arm straight and to
keep one foot on the tape when he or she turned. If any item fell or
started to fall, the trial ended. The examiner made a comment such as
"Oh dear" or "That was a hard one" or "Maybe next time," and the
failure was noted on the score card. If the child succeeded, he or she was
verbally reinforced, the success was noted on the score card, and the
appropriate number of tokens were placed next to the token dish. The
instructions for the subsequent five trials were: "Pick your second
(third, fourth, etc.) box from any bag you want." The child was
informed when he or she had fulfilled the criteria for winning the
certificate.

After all six trials were completed, the child counted his or her tokens
and chose the toy(s) he or she had won. The certificate, if won, was kept
by the examiner and shown to the principal and teacher before being
given to the child.

On each trial, the level of difficulty that the child attempted and his or
her success or failure were recorded. Both factors were taken into
account in the development of a scoring system to measure the amount
of risk that the child was willing to take. Further, if a child succeeded on
an attempt and chose to make his or her next attempt at the same level
of difficulty, the child was considered to be risking less than a child who
dared to increase the level he or she attempted on the next trial.

Similarly, a successful child who stayed on level was considered to risk less than a child who failed but nevertheless tried again to master the same level of difficulty. Based on this reasoning, the scoring system devised gave greater weight to upward changes following failure than to upward changes following success, and lesser penalties to downward changes following failure than to downward changes following success.

The child's total risk score was computed as follows. The first trial choice of either the "easy," "little hard," or "very hard" task was assigned a score of 1, 2, or 3, respectively. On the following five trials, the directions of the child's choice of difficulty level (up or down from the trial completed) following success or failure was scored. Considering all possible choices, the level of change from one trial to another can be *described* as +2 (moves up 2 levels), +1 (moves up 1 level), 0 (stays at same level), –1 (drops 1 level), and –2 (drops 2 levels). These level changes were then assigned scores of +6, +4, +1, 0, and –1 respectively if such change followed a successful trial, and scores of +8, +6, +4, +1, and 0, respectively, following failure. Since the child's first trial followed neither success nor failure, he or she was simply given a score for this trial equal to the level of difficulty which he or she attempted. This first value plus the five-level-change scores for the subsequent trials yielded the child's total risk score. The possible scores, then, ranged from a low risk score of 6 to a high risk score of 25.

It is recognized that this risk score is somewhat cumbersome and arbitrary. Pilot worked showed that it also was correlated to a significant degree with the simple number of successes. Nevertheless, the risk score, rather than number of successes, was retained for analysis because it seemed better to reflect the child's style of approaching a problem. Two additional scores were analyzed: the first difficulty level attempted, which was assumed to reflect a generalized level of self-confidence independent of experience with the specific task; and the mean difficulty level attempted. In total, then, three scores were obtained from the Balancing game: (1) first level tried; (2) mean level tried; and (3) risk score.

Reading Game. The Reading game was developed to parallel the Balancing game. In this task, however, the child was confronted with an academic task. As in the Balancing game, the child was presented with several opportunities to choose to perform tasks which varied in difficulty level.

Three decorated shoe boxes labeled "easy," "a little hard," and "very hard," each containing 10 sentence cards, were employed for the task.

Printed on the "easy" cards were sentences composed of first-grade words. The box considered to be "a little hard" contained sentence cards at the child's grade level (either second or third), and the "very hard" sentences included words at the fifth- and sixth-grade reading levels. The level of word difficulty was based upon the Scott Foresman reading series word lists. Other materials employed were the following: a certificate that the child could win during the game, a score card including the "rules" for winning a certificate and toys, 30 plastic tokens, and a box of assorted small toys.

The examiner sat at the table to the right of the child and began the session by putting the boxes on the table along with the certificate and score card. The task was explained as follows:

> Now we're going to play a word game. Each of these boxes will have some sentence cards in it. In this box I'll put easy sentences like this one [examiner showed the sample card to the child and read it]. In this box the sentences are a little harder, like this one [showed and read sample], and the sentences in this box are very hard [showed and read the sample]. Now, let me tell you how to play the game. You will have six turns to read sentences from any box you want. If you read four sentences with no mistakes by the end of the game, you will win a special certificate that your teacher and principal will see [read the certificate to the child]. Now, you will be able to win some prizes in this game, too. Each time you read a sentence from the easy box without any mistakes, I'll give you one of these tokens. I'll give you three tokens when you read a sentence without any mistakes from the little hard box, and you'll get five tokens if you read a sentence from the very hard box with no mistakes. Now, you can buy any of these toys with your tokens, but each toy costs five tokens, so the more tokens you have, the more toys you can get, OK? Let's use this score card so it will be easier to remember [showed child the card]. See, you have six turns. Every time you read a sentence without a mistake, I'll put a check mark here. If you read four sentences from *any* box without a mistake, you get the certificate, but the number of toys you get depends upon the box you choose. All right? Pick a sentence.

The instructions for the subsequent five trials were: "Pick your second (third, fourth, etc.) sentence from any box you want." After each trial the examiner recorded the child's choice, filled in the score card, and gave the child the appropriate number of tokens if the sentence had been read correctly. Verbal reinforcement was given for each correct sentence.

At the end of the game, the child counted his or her tokens and chose the toy(s) he or she had won. The certificate, if won, was kept by the examiner to be shown to the principal and classroom teacher before being given to the child.

The Reading game was parallel in form to the Balancing game, differing only in content. As with the Balancing game, the level of difficulty attempted and the success or failure were recorded for each of the six trials. The first level attempted, the mean level attempted, and the risk score were used as self-confidence measures.

Autonomy Measures

Find-the-Surprise Game. A single task, "Find-the-Surprise," was employed as a measure of autonomy. Like the verbal creativity tasks, the autonomy task was administered on more than one occasion during the testing session.

The Find-the-Surprise game was constructed to appear as a game of chance that could be interpreted by the child as a problem to be solved. The child was presented with an ambiguous choice situation, as well as reports of how others behaved when confronted with the task. It was assumed that imitative behavior in such a situation reflects a general belief that others, compared to oneself, are more adequate in their problem-solving behavior.

The materials for the first administration of the task consisted of a 12 cm × 10.8 cm × 8.9 cm colored cardboard chest with four drawers labeled A, B, C, and D. Inside each lettered drawer was a small rubber ball. The examiner placed the chest of drawers on the table in front of the child and said:

> See these four drawers? In this game you'll get to pick the drawer you want to open. There's a surprise inside each one. You know something? We don't play this game just with kids; we play it with grownups, too. And before we start to play, I'm going to tell you which drawers other people picked, and then you can choose whichever drawer you want to open. Now, you can have the surprise inside, so remember, you can open any drawer you want. But, when we played this game with *kids your age*, most of *them* opened drawer A [examiner pointed], but most *grownups* opened drawer C [examiner pointed]. Which one, *any one,* do *you* want to open?

On the second administration, the materials consisted of a 29.2 cm × 14.6 cm × 8.9 cm colored shoe box sectioned into four compartments with doors along one side. The four doors were labeled A, B, C, and D. A marble was placed inside each lettered compartment. For the third administration, the materials consisted of four aluminum tubs, 10.2 cm in diameter and 5.1 cm high, with plastic lids covered with colored paper. The four tubs were labeled A, B, C, and D, and each contained a plastic jumping bean. For the fourth administration, four green cotton drawstring bags, 10.2 cm × 7.6 cm, were used. Each of the bags was lettered and each contained a small plastic airplane. The administration and task instructions were similar in the second through fourth administration to the instructions given when the task was first introduced. The specific letters designated as the favorite drawer of other children and of adults were changed across the four trials.

The child's choice of alternatives was recorded for each of the four presentations. The total number of autonomous choices (choices of neither the peers' nor the adults' favorite alternative) was used as an autonomy score. Since the child's reaction to the first presentation was uninfluenced by prior reinforcement effects and by experience with the task, the first trial performance (imitative versus autonomous) was also used as a score.

Curiosity Measure

Opening Doors Game. A single task was employed to measure curiosity. The "Opening Doors" task, originally developed by Harter and Zigler (1974) to measure a child's curiosity for novel stimuli, consists of giving the child a series of opportunities to choose between a known and a novel picture. It was assumed that the choice to vary the stimulus field reflects the child's exploratory behavior.

The task materials consisted of 18 house-like stimuli, constructed from manila folders 22.2 cm from peak to base and 29.8 cm in width when folded. Each stimulus had two doors which could be unfolded to reveal pictures drawn directly behind them "inside the house." When the doors were folded, the inside pictures were not visible. On one of the two doors of each house was drawn a picture which was identical to the picture behind the door. On the other outside door there was no picture; behind this blank door, however, was a picture different from those on the other side of the house. The position of the blank door (left or right) was varied across stimulus presentations. The examiner explained the task as follows:

> Here are some houses. See, each of these houses has two doors. On one door there will be a picture and on the other door, nothing. It will be blank. Now, there will also be pictures behind both doors. Behind the

door with the picture on it will always be another picture just like it [examiner opened door and pointed], but the picture behind the blank door will always be a different picture [opened door and pointed]. What you get to do in this game is to pick the door that *you* want to open so that you can look at the picture behind it, OK? Before we start, let's look at another house. Which door has the same picture and which door has a different picture behind it? Right. Let's look at one more house before we start. Which door has the same picture behind it? Good. Which one has a different picture? Good. OK, let's begin. Pick whichever door *you want to open* and look at the picture behind it.

The curiosity measure was the total number of blank doors chosen on the 15 trials that followed the three demonstration trials. Prior use of this measure with 83 fourth-grade disadvantaged children has resulted in an alternate form test–retest reliability coefficient of .56; for a sample of 72 advantaged fourth-grade children the reliability coefficient was .40 (Seitz, 1974).

Frustration Threshold Measures

The length of time which elapsed before the child made a frustration statement on the Dog and Bone game previously described was taken as one measure of a child's frustration threshold. Another measure from a previously described task was the total number of attempts the child made to remove the token from the box in the Token-in-the-Box game.

Puzzle Game.   The Puzzle game was designed to measure both the child's frustration threshold and his or her degree of independence when solving a complex problem. The task requires the child to attempt to complete an extremely difficult puzzle with no help from the examiner.

Two plywood puzzles were employed for the task. The first puzzle consisted of eight multicolored triangular and trapezoidal pieces. Assembled correctly, the pieces formed a square which fit on a 33 cm × 33 cm square of black cardboard. The puzzle was extremely difficult, and pilot testing had indicated that it was highly improbable that a child could solve it within the time limits provided. A second simple puzzle was also administered, although not scored, in order to reduce the child's sense of failure with the first puzzle. The second puzzle consisted of 12 multicolored and multishaped pieces which also fit on the black cardboard base. When assembled, the simple puzzle depicted a six-pointed star.

The examiner presented the first puzzle saying: "Let's play another game. Here's an easy puzzle for you to do. It shouldn't take too long to put together, but if you get sick of working on it, you can stop whenever you want to; just tell me. Put it together so that when it is all finished, it will fit onto this piece of paper here [examiner pointed to black cardboard]."

While the child attempted to assemble the puzzle, the examiner recorded all verbal statements. No reinforcement was given, and if the examiner was asked any direct questions she replied by saying, "I'm afraid I can't help you."

After 3 minutes had elapsed or when the child wanted to stop working on the puzzle, the examiner looked at the puzzle and said: "You know, something doesn't look right about that puzzle. Wait a minute. [Thumbed through pages of data sheets as if checking.] O dear! That puzzle's for sixth-graders. Here's the puzzle you should have gotten. [Examiner gave the second puzzle to the child and removed the first.] You shouldn't have any trouble with this one." The examiner then gave the child any help that was needed, and she concluded by saying, "Good. That was a lot more fun, wasn't it?"

Only performance on the first difficult puzzle was scored. As a measure of frustration threshold, the total length of time which the child spent trying to complete the puzzle was recorded. The child's verbal statements were also recorded and were scored for dependency, as described below.

Dependency Measures

Three tasks were employed to measure dependency: the Walk-the-Board, Puzzle, and Five-Objects tasks.

One dependency measure was obtained from the previously described Puzzle game. The verbal statements made while the child was attempting to solve the puzzle were scored for verbal dependency using the Gewirtz (1954) scoring system. Four categories of responses were recorded: (1) egocentric comments, such as the child's talking to himself or herself; (2) declarative statements that do not call for an actual reply but which demand attention (e.g., "This is really hard."); (3) simple questions or requests for information; and (4) verbal requests calling for more than information (e.g., asking for help, praise, or direct attention). The total number of statements in groups (3) and (4) was divided by the total time worked in order to provide a score of verbal dependency statements per unit of time worked.

Walk-the-Board Game. This task was adapted from a similar task developed by Heathers (1953) to measure a child's independence or dependence in a situation involving the threat of physical harm. There was, of course, no actual danger to the child, but the child's illusion of threat was heightened by the use of a blindfold during the task. (It deserves comment that although the children frequently performed the task in a dependent and somewhat fearful manner, it was almost unanimously chosen to be the "most favorite game" in the battery.) Only the physical expression of dependency rather than verbal requests for help were scored on this measure. In prior work with the task, Heathers found some evidence that independent performance on the task was related to aspects of the home life of the child, such as a less child-centered home and a high degree of demands for accelerated performance made upon the child.

The apparatus consisted of two 1.8-m-long × 30.5-cm-wide wooden planks. One plank served as a baseboard upon which was attached a centrally located fulcrum and, at either end, two large coil springs. The second plank was placed above the baseboard and attached to springs which served to raise it approximately 20.3 cm from the floor. The springs and the fulcrum acted to provide instability to the top plank which tipped sidewise as well as endwise when weight was placed on it. A weight of approximately 60 pounds applied to the end of the plank was required to tip the plank to the floor. For safety purposes, 2.5-cm-high sideboards were placed on the plank to prevent stepping off the side, and a small strip of wood was nailed across one end of the plank in order to alert the child that he or she was near the end.

Prior to the presentation of this task, the child was at no time permitted to inspect or test the apparatus in any way. The following introduction to the task was presented while the child and examiner were seated at the table with their backs to the apparatus:

> In the next game you get to walk along a Wiggly Board. That sounds like fun, huh? Well, my game company wants to know whether kids can do this blindfolded. You sit here while I put the blindfold on you, and then we'll try it.

A black scarf was used to blindfold the child, who was then led to the apparatus. The instructions continued:

> Now, what you have to do is walk the Wiggly Board till you get to one end, and you'll know when you've reached that end because your toe will bump against a board. Then turn around and walk back. Keep walking

till I say stop, then *step* down to the floor, *don't jump* down. Now, we know this might be pretty scary, so I'll always have my hand close to yours, and, if you want to, you can hold it as you walk along the board, OK?

The experimenter helped the child step onto the board and faced him or her in the right direction. Before the child started to walk, the experimenter touched the child's hand in order to give him or her and opportunity to hold. Whether or not the child took the experimenter's hand, she walked along next to the child in order to catch the child should he or she lose his or her balance. During each trial, the experimenter touched the child's hand two or three times so that the child could take it if he or she wished.

Three trials were given in immediate succession. Each trial consisted of three behaviors: walking the board once, turning around, and walking the board again. The child was led to the starting end and helped into the starting position after each trial. On each trial the helping hand was offered in the same way as on the first trial. No child was urged to walk the board if she or he refused.

The score for the task was based on the number of times in three trials that the child held the examiner's hand, used the examiner's hand to maintain his or her balance, or refused to walk at all. Each segment of each trial, walking to the end, turning around, and walking back to the beginning, was given a score of 0, 1, 2, or 3. A score of 0 was given if the child walked without using the offered hand, a score of 1 if the child held it only halfway or used it only to steady himself or herself if he or she began to lose his or her balance, a score of 2 if the child held the hand, and a score of 3 if the child refused. Total scores for the nine segments could thus range from 0, or completely independent, to 27, or refusal to walk the board at all.

Five-Objects Game. The purpose of the Five-Objects task was to assess the child's performance in an ambiguous problem-solving situation in which his or her solutions were met with repeated failure. In contrast to the Puzzle and the Token-in-the-Box measures, the solution to the Five-Objects task was not determined by the structure of the task, and the child was required to ask whether he or she had successfully solved the problem. The child was consistently informed that his or her proposed solution was not the correct one. The tendency of the child to repeatedly rely on his or her own resources to solve the problem was the variable of interest.

The materials for the task consisted of: a ballpoint pen, a straightened paper clip, a 7.6 cm × 10.2 cm × 1.3 cm block with a small hole in it, a small kleenex, and a piece of rubber tubing. The examiner placed the articles on the table in front of the child and said:

> See all this? Now, you can do all kinds of things with this stuff. For example, you could put this on here [examiner put the tubing on the pen] and stick it in here [examiner placed pen in the block of wood]. Now the problem is, there's only one *right* thing to do, and what I just did wasn't right. If *you* do the right thing, you get to choose another toy. Now, you only have 3 minutes, so every time you think you might have done the right thing and you want me to check it, *tell* me, and if you are right, you get a toy. Remember, you've got to tell me every time you want me to see if you've got the answer, OK? You have 3 minutes. Go ahead.

Two measures were recorded for the Five-Objects game: (a) the total number of correctness inquiries made; and (b) whether the child required prompting to give his or her final solution. As previously noted, the largest number of objects employed by the child was used as a creativity measure.

CHILDREN'S INTERVIEWS

Self-Concept Interview

The self-concept interview was an adaptation of the Brown Self-Concept Scale (1966), designed for use with both black and white children. The interview was introduced in the following manner: "Now, as I told you earlier, the game company I work for wants to make games that boys and girls like, and we'd like to know more about kids your age so we can make better games. That's why we ask them questions about themselves. Now I'd like to ask *you* some questions about yourself, about (child's name), OK?"

The child was then read a 14-item questionnaire, which included such questions as whether the child was happy or sad, good or bad, smart or dumb. The questions were phrased as follows: "Is (child's name) happy or is (he or she) sad?" (A copy of the questionnaire is included in Appendix A.) No reinforcement was given during the task. Each question was scored 1 for a positive response and 0 for a negative response.

Perception of Teacher's View Interview ("Teacher Thinks")

The same items described for the self-concept interview were asked again, except the questions were rephrased to state, for example, "Does (teacher's name) think (child's name) is happy or does she think he (or she) is sad?" This portion of the interview was also adapted from a similar procedure employed by Brown (1966). The examiner introduced the interview as follows: "Now I'd like to ask you some more questions. This time I'd like to ask you a few questions about your teacher. What's her name? Now, do *you* suppose that (teacher's name) thinks. . . ." Each question was scored 1 for a positive response and 0 for a negative response.

TEACHER RATING SCALE

Teachers were asked to rate each child on 12 attributes: creativity, curiosity, popularity with peers, neatness, independence, maturity, persistence, classroom achievement, reading ability, leadership, fearfulness of people, and fearfulness of things in general. All ratings were made on a 7-point scale, and the teachers were asked to rate the child relative to other children in the same classroom. A score of 7 represented the maximum positive direction for a trait (e.g, creative, not afraid of other people). The sum of the 12 ratings could range from 12 to 84, with higher numbers indicating more favorable ratings. It should be noted that only six children, all of whom were advantaged black children, had a classroom teacher who was black. All other teachers in the study were white.

SCHOOL ACHIEVEMENT

Reading and arithmetic achievement scores from standardized school achievement tests were obtained from school records for most children in both studies. The test scores were recorded in terms of grade and month equivalencies (e.g., second grade, fifth month). The type of test, the grade, and the month when the child was tested were also noted. The scores were adjusted for time of testing in the present study by assuming a normal growth rate of one month's achievement per month of school (computed on a 10-month school year). Thus, if the child was seen six

3 Results

For purposes of clarity, the results are presented in seven sections. In the first section, the relationships among the performance measures within and between construct areas are examined. In the next two sections, results are presented for the measures obtained directly from the children: their performance on the experimental tasks, and their responses to the interviews. The relationship between the teachers' ratings and the children's behavior and verbal responses is examined in section four. In sections five and six, two factors, father's presence or absence and the racial composition of the schools, are presented in terms of their relationships with both the children's and the teachers' response measures. The findings from the school achievement data, available from school records, and other nonexperimental background data are presented in the final section.

PERFORMANCE MEASURES AND CONSTRUCT RELATIONSHIPS

As described in the previous chapter, the tasks designed for the present studies were intended to measure six construct areas: creativity, self-confidence, autonomy, curiosity, frustration threshold, and dependency. Cronbach and Meehl (1955) have pointed out that tests which presume to measure the same construct should correlate more highly with each other than with those tests which measure some other construct. The matrix of intercorrelations among the experimental school months following the administration of the achievement test, months were added to his or her recorded achievement score. It recognized that such a procedure penalizes high-achieving students a overestimates the probable achievement of low-achieving students, l this procedure seemed the best available for rendering the existi achievement scores approximately comparable for all children.

measures for the 304 children who participated in the two studies is presented in Table 3.1. (Data from the questionnaire responses and from the teacher rating scale are included in this table for the sake of economy of presentation, even though they are not discussed in the present section.)

A factor analysis of the correlation matrix shown in Table 3.1 did not produce a particularly useful solution, with the first eight factors accounting for only 58% of the variance. As may be seen in Table 3.1, intratask correlations were generally much higher than intertask correlations, and this fact spelled itself out in the tendency for the factors which were identified to be task-specific. Rather than employing factor analysis, therefore, evidence for the existence of underlying constructs was sought simply by examining whether measures which were hypothesized to be related were in fact related to a statistically significant degree.

Creativity

As can be seen in Table 3.1, the strength of the interrelationships among the tasks designed to measure creativity varied. The most significant relationships were among the three measures of high originality: High originality on the Verbal Creativity tasks was significantly related to measures of originality (quality) on the Dog and Bone and Token-in-the-Box tasks. There is thus some evidence that originality was a measurable trait which was not restricted to a single type of task. The fluency and flexibility measures were related to several other measures, with the common feature appearing to be a general talkativeness: For example, children highly fluent on the Verbal Creativity tasks made more dependency statements on the Puzzle, and they made a frustration statement sooner than did other children on the Dog and Bone task. To some extent, the failure to find a relationship between the fluency measure and other creativity measures appeared to be a function of the scores employed. That is, in all cases measures of originality were corrected for the overall number of responses made. The fluency score, however, was highly correlated with the total originality score before dividing by the number of responses ($r = .82$). Of the four tasks employed to measure creativity, only one, the Five-Objects task, appeared not to do so. The highest number of objects used in the Five-Objects task was unrelated to any other measure of creativity. Overall, the relationship among the verbal creativity measures was stronger than the relationship among the nonverbal creativity measures. In general,

TABLE 3.1
Correlations Among Experimental Measures for All Children Tested in the Matched Groups and Typical Groups Studies (N = 304)

	Verbal Creativity			Dog & Bone		Token-in-the-Box		Five-Objects	Reading			Balancing		
	Highest originality	Fluency	Flexibility	Quality per path	Highest quality	Quality per attempt	Highest quality	Highest number	First attempt	Mean attempt	Risk	First attempt	Mean attempt	Risk
Verbal Creativity:														
Originality per response	.72**	−.19**	.05	.21**	.21**	.09	.11	−.02	.16**	.20**	−.04	−.07	.07	.12*
Highest originality		.10	.46**	.18**	.22**	.09	.15**	.05	.09	.05	−.09	.01	.03	.03
Fluency			.48**	.04	.09	−.08	−.02	.10	−.07	−.14*	.02	.09	.08	.01
Flexibility				.09	.13*	.02	.10	.09	−.02	−.08	.01	.14*	.01	−.05
Dog and Bone:														
Quality per path					.77**	.06	.00	.02	.12*	.16**	.07	−.01	.19**	.17**
Highest quality						−.01	−.03	.02	.12*	.12*	.09	.01	.16**	.14*
Token-in-the-Box:														
Quality per attempt							.66**	.03	.02	.02	.02	−.06	.07	.11
Highest quality·								.00	−.03	−.02	−.02	−.00	−.02	−.01
Five-Objects:														
Highest number									.03	−.04	−.06	.03	−.02	−.07
Reading:														
First attempt										.61**	−.05	.24**	.21**	.04
Mean attempt											.44**	.16**	.36**	.20**
Risk												−.04	.21**	.21**
Balancing:														
First attempt													.24**	.16**
Mean attempt														.58**
Risk														
Token-in-the-Box:														
Expectancy of success														
Find-the-Surprise														
First choice														
Total autonomous responses														
Opening Doors:														
Number blank														
Dog and Bone:														
Time to frustration														
Token-in-the-Box:														
Number of attempts														
Puzzle:														
Total time														
Walk-the-Board:														
Handholding requests														
Puzzle:														
Number of dependency statements														
Five-Objects:														
Requests for feedback														
Needed prompting														
Self-Concept:														
Total score														
Teacher thinks:														
Total score														

*p < .05.
**p < .01.

TABLE 3.1 *(continued)*

Token-in-the-Box	Find-the-Surprise		Opening Doors	Dog & Bone	Token-in-in-the-Box	Puzzle	Walk-the-Board	Puzzle	Five-Objects		Self-Concept	Teacher Thinks	Teacher Ratings
Expectancy of success	First choice	Total autonomous responses	Number blank	Time to frustration	Number of attempts	Total time	Handholding requests	Number of dependency statements	Requests for feedback	Needed prompting	Total score	Total score	Total score
.09	-.02	-.10	.23**	-.11	.04	-.05	-.17**	.03	.06	-.02	.07	.02	.20**
.07	-.04	-.04	.08	-.17**	.08	-.04	-.14*	.08	.12*	.05	.07	.05	.13*
-.07	.03	.10	-.25**	-.16**	.08	-.11	.04	.24**	.11	.10	.03	.06	-.14*
-.05	-.03	.02	-.12*	-.11*	.07	.04	.01	.10	.13*	.09	.08	.11	-.10
.00	.08	.06	.11	.16**	-.02	.03	-.10	.09	.00	.02	.08	.08	.12*
.00	-.02	-.02	.10	.12*	-.03	.03	-.07	.11	-.01	-.10	.13*	.02	.14*
.12*	-.07	-.02	.04	.01	-.02	.01	-.10	-.12*	-.02	-.11*	-.01	.03	.02
.24**	-.09	.01	.08	.02	.25**	.17**	-.06	-.08	-.01	-.09	.06	.06	-.01
.04	-.02	.06	-.06	.02	-.01	.02	-.02	.04	-.14*	-.16**	-.08	-.07	-.04
-.06	.07	.09	.20**	-.03	-.11	-.02	-.06	-.11	-.03	.12*	-.01	.00	.22**
-.02	.13*	.12*	.20**	.07	-.07	-.05	-.02	-.09	-.02	.07	.02	.00	.35**
.00	.13*	.12*	-.01	.08	-.03	.05	-.03	.05	.06	-.01	-.06	.00	.08
.06	.06	.12*	-.03	-.10	.09	.14*	-.07	.05	.00	.08	.01	.02	-.05
.03	-.00	-.02	.11*	.02	.05	.00	-.11	-.01	.02	.04	-.02	.04	-.04
-.07	.03	-.01	.16**	.05	-.12*	-.01	-.06	-.09	.02	.00	-.01	.01	-.08
	-.11	-.06	-.04	-.04	.24**	.11	-.11*	-.08	.01	.01	.01	-.06	-.05
		.70**	-.06	.08	-.10	.10	-.02	.04	.10	.06	.01	-.02	-.01
		-.06	.05	.02	.07	-.04	.11	.05	-.03	.00	-.02	-.01
				-.04	.01	.07	-.07	-.07	.06	.14*	-.02	.01	.13*
					.06	.13*	-.02	-.20**	-.14*	.11*	.01	-.08	-.05
						.24**	.01	-.04	.03	.05	-.09	-.05	-.04
							.04	-.40**	-.06	.09	-.03	-.10	-.04
								-.01	.02	-.06	-.02	-.06	.11
									.15*	-.17**	.04	.16**	.03
										-.31**	-.05	.10	.04
											.05	.00	-.01
												.46**	.06
													-.10

there was reasonably good evidence to suggest the existence of an underlying trait of creativity which was tapped by three of the four tasks employed for that purpose.

Self-Confidence

Two of the three tasks employed to measure confidence—the Reading and Balancing tasks—were significantly related. The relationship found between these two tasks suggests a consistency of response to both nonacademic and academic problem situations. It was also generally the case that measures on these two tasks were more closely related to each other than to measures from other tasks, although to some degree they were related to measures of creativity and curiosity. The third task measure, intended to assess a child's confidence in his or her ability to succeed on the Token-in-the-Box task, was unrelated to the other self-confidence measures.

Autonomy

As only a single task was employed to assess autonomy, cross-method trait correlations could not be determined. Responses to this task were generally unrelated to responses to other tasks, although a few correlations with the self-confidence measures attained significance at the .05 level.

Curiosity

As with the autonomy trait, only a single task was employed to measure curiosity. While the Opening Doors task has been used in other research on children's curiosity (Harter & Zigler, 1974; Kreitler, Zigler, & Kreitler, 1975) and has in some cases been taken as an operational definition of the trait, in the present studies it was related both to the self-confidence and the creativity measures. Although the Opening Doors task may be a valid measure of curiosity, the trait of curiosity did not appear to be independent of other traits examined in the present investigation.

Frustration Threshold

The amount of time the child spent on the complex Puzzle game was significantly and positively related to the number of attempts she or he made to remove the token from the box and to the length of time before she or he made a frustration statement on the Dog and Bone task. There is thus some indication that frustration threshold constitutes a trait that was consistently expressed across three tasks with somewhat differing demands. There was also some evidence that the child who persisted longer in problem solving was less verbally dependent.

Dependency

Two of the three tasks employed to assess dependency, the Puzzle and the Five-Objects tasks, were significantly related. Children who made many dependency statements on the Puzzle task also made more requests for feedback on the Five-Objects task and were unlikely to require prompting before asking if their solution was correct. The hand-holding score from the Walk-the-Board game was not related to the verbal requests for help in the other two tasks.

In summary, there was reasonable indication that the traits of creativity, self-confidence, frustration threshold, and dependency were measured by the tasks employed in the present investigation, although the traits were not totally independent of each other. The traits of autonomy and curiosity were each measured by a single task; thus, a multimethod analysis could not be applied.

CHILDREN'S PERFORMANCE MEASURES

The large number of dependent variables and the significant correlations among them required that the data be analyzed by multivariate analyses of variance. Those variables of a dichotomous rather than a continuous nature were not included in the multivariate analysis but were examined by chi-square analyses. These were: (1) confidence in ability to succeed on the Token-in-the-Box task; (2) need for prompting on the Five-Objects game; and (3) imitative or autonomous initial response on the Find-the-Surprise task.

An adjustment in the scoring procedures was necessary for some children whose performance on two of the tasks was unexpected. The "number of attempts" on the Token-in-the-Box task was meant to measure persistence on a complex task presumed to be unsolvable and was, therefore, inappropriate for children who solved the problem. Surprisingly, eight children in the matched groups and 13 in the typical groups study did so. These successful children were distributed approximately equally across the different groups of the studies, and there was no relationship between any of the independent variables investigated and success on this task. The successful children were therefore given a score on this measure equal to the mean number of attempts made by the unsuccessful children in their same group. The second measure that had to be adjusted was the risk score on the Reading task. For three children in the matched groups study and seven in the typical groups study, no score was calculated because the task was either too easy for the child (four or more successes following attempts at the hardest level) or too hard (four or more failures following attempts at the easiest level). These children were assigned risk score values equal to the mean value for the remaining children in their group. No more than two children in any one group were affected by this adjustment. Of the 10 instances, eight were for high levels of success rather than failure.

Matched Groups Study

The 23 continuous dependent variables were analyzed by an SES × Race × Sex multivariate analysis of variance with two levels per factor and 12 subjects per cell. A significant multivariate main effect for SES was found, $F(23,66) = 2.10$, $p < .01$. None of the remaining main effects or interactions was significant. In the follow-up analyses to determine which of the individual measures contributed to the significant overall SES effect, 4 of the 23 dependent measures were found to have a significant univariate F-value for the SES main effect. Table 3.2 presents the means entering into these significant findings. (A complete table of the means for each group on each measure is presented in Appendix B.)

As can be seen in Table 3.2 economically advantaged children scored significantly higher than economically disadvantaged children on the highest level of response generated on the Token-in-the-Box task. Likewise, on the Reading task, advantaged children chose significantly harder problems, both on their first attempt and across all attempts at the task. On the Puzzle task, disadvantaged children made significantly more dependency statements to the examiner per length of time they spent on the task.

The three noncontinuous measures, expectancy for success, need for prompting, and autonomous choice, were analyzed by SES × Race × Sex partitioned chi-square analyses (Winer, 1971). For each of the three analyses, the overall chi-square value was not significant. Further analyses of the data were therefore not performed.

TABLE 3.2
Significant SES Effects Found in the Analyses of Children's Performance in the
Matched Groups Study

| | | Performance | | | |
| | | Advantaged | | Disadvantaged | |
Dependent Measure	Univariate F-Value and Probability	$\bar{X}$	SD	$\bar{X}$	SD
Token-in-the-Box:					
Highest quality	$F(1,88) = 8.75, p < .01$	6.25	.95	5.35	1.81
Reading:					
First attempt	$F(1,88) = 10.56, p < .01$	1.83	.72	1.38	.62
Mean attempt	$F(1,88) = 4.62, p < .05$	1.83	.39	1.66	.40
Puzzle:					
Dependency statements per minute	$F(1,88) = 4.07, p < .05$	.18	.33	.36	.49

Typical Groups Study

As had been done for the matched groups study, the 23 continuous dependent variables for the typical sample were analyzed by an SES × Race × Sex multivariate analysis of variance, with two levels for each of the factors and 20 subjects per cell. Significant multivariate main effects were found for SES, $F(23,130) = 4.90, p < .001$, and for race, $F(23,130) = 1.82, p < .05$. No other significant main effects or interactions were found. The significant univariate findings for SES and for race are shown in Table 3.3. (A complete table of means for each group on every measure is given in Appendix C.)

Almost half of the 23 dependent variables showed significant univariate F-values for the SES main effect. As can be seen in Table 3.3, the direction of these findings was mixed. Disadvantaged children were more fluent and flexible on the Verbal Creativity tasks, showed more autonomy on the Five-Objects task, and chose a more difficult task level when they first attempted the Balancing game. Advantaged children showed higher quality and originality per response on the Dog and Bone and Verbal Creativity tasks, made fewer dependency statements on the Puzzle task, showed more curiosity on the Opening Doors task, and chose a more difficult task level both on their first attempt and across all attempts on the Reading task.

Despite the significant main effect for race, only two of the 23 continuous variables showed significant univariate F-values. White

TABLE 3.3
Significant SES and Race Effects Found in the Analyses of
Children's Performance in the Typical Groups Study

		Performance			
		Advantaged		Disadvantaged	
Dependent Measure	Univariate F-Value and Probability	$\bar{X}$	SD	$\bar{X}$	SD
SES Effects					
Verbal Creativity:					
Originality per response	$F(1,152) = 14.18, p < .001$	3.12	.76	2.69	.67
Fluency	$F(1,152) = 10.36, p < .01$	8.15	4.15	10.28	4.23
Flexibility	$F(1,152) = 8.49, p < .01$	3.58	1.52	4.37	1.84
Dog and Bone:					
Quality per path	$F(1,152) = 9.03, p < .01$	1.32	.51	1.09	.49
Reading:					
First attempt	$F(1,152) = 20.31, p < .001$	1.79	.76	1.30	.58
Mean attempt	$F(1,152) = 20.26, p < .001$	1.95	.49	1.65	.34
Balancing:					
First attempt	$F(1,152) = 5.41, p < .05$	1.71	.73	2.00	.84
Opening Doors:					
Number blank	$F(1,152) = 8.87, p < .01$	9.64	3.34	7.75	4.51
Puzzle:					
Dependency statements per minute	$F(1,152) = 7.51, p < .01$	.30	.48	.54	.50
Five-Objects:					
Requests for feedback	$F(1,152) = 5.79, p < .05$	4.24	3.19	5.89	5.29
Race Effects		Black		White	
Find-the-Surprise:					
Total autonomous responses	$F(1,152) = 4.31, p < .05$	2.38	1.10	2.79	1.19
Token-in-the-Box:					
Number of attempts	$F(1,152) = 5.21, p < .05$	17.61	7.45	20.44	8.34

children made more attempts to solve the Token-in-the-Box problem
and more autonomous choices on the Find-the-Surprise measure.

In the SES × Race × Sex partitioned chi-square analyses of the
dichotomized variables, the overall chi-square value was significant for
the need-for-prompting variable on the Five-Objects task. Follow-up
analyses revealed that advantaged white children were more likely to

require prompting than were any other group of children: Prompting was required for 28% of the advantaged white children and only 3% of the remaining children, $\chi^2(3) = 21.99$, $p < .001$.

Covariance Analyses.   Because many of the groups of children in the typical groups study differed significantly in MA and IQ (see Table 3.3), several covariance analyses were performed in order to statistically hold constant the effects of these variables. One of the major interests in performing these analyses was to compare the results with those from the procedure, employed in the first study, of controlling the IQ and MA variables by direct matching. With both methods, the purpose is to determine whether SES, race, and sex differences on the dependent measures are independent of those differences associated with MA and IQ. The comparison of the results of the matched groups study with the results of the covariance analyses for the typical groups study will be discussed more fully in the next chapter.

Three separate multivariate analyses of covariance were performed. The first of these analyses was an SES × Race × Sex multivariate analysis of covariance of the 23 dependent variables with IQ as a covariate. The second was an identical analysis except that the covariate was MA. In the third analysis both IQ and MA were covariates. Table 3.4 summarizes the results of these three analyses.

As can be seen in Tables 3.3 and 3.4, the SES effects in the original multivariate analysis remained nearly unchanged when IQ and MA were covaried. The multivariate main effect for SES was consistently significant across all four analyses, although there were some minor changes in the univariate *F*-values. Two variables, the Dog and Bone quality per path and the curiosity score, which had significantly differentiated between the advantaged and disadvantaged groups in the original analysis, no longer did so when either IQ or MA was a covariate. Reading risk, which had not been significantly different across social classes in the original analysis, was significant when the effects of IQ, or of IQ and MA jointly, were statistically controlled: Disadvantaged children had significantly higher risk scores than did advantaged children.

The covariance analyses produced substantially different results for the race variable compared to the SES variable. The effect of race, which was significant in the original analysis, was no longer significant in any of the covariance analyses. As in the original analysis, there was no main effect for sex, and none of the interactions was significant in any of the covariance analyses.

TABLE 3.4

Summary of Results of Three SES × Race × Sex Multivariate Analyses of Covariance of Children's Performance Measures for the Typical Groups Study[a]

Effect	Multivariate Effects			Measure	Univariate Effects		
	IQ as Covariate	MA as Covariate	IQ & MA as Covariates		IQ as Covariate	MA as Covariate	IQ & MA as Covariates
SES	<.002	<.002	<.001	Verbal creativity:			
				Originality per response	<.05	<.02	<.05
				Fluency	<.05	<.001	<.02
				Flexibility	<.01	<.001	<.001
				Dog and Bone:			
				Quality per path	—	—	—
				Reading:			
				First attempt	<.05	<.001	<.02
				Mean attempt	<.05	<.01	<.05
				[Risk]	<.02	—	<.05
				Balancing:			
				First attempt	<.05	<.01	<.02
				Opening Doors:			
				Number blank	—	—	—
				Puzzle:			
				Dependency statements	<.05	<.02	<.05
				Five-Objects:			
				Requests for feedback	<.05	<.02	<.05
Race	—	—	—				

[a]The nonbracketed measures listed in this table are all of the measures for which significant SES findings were obtained in the original multivariate analysis of the typical groups data. The bracketed measure attained significance only after the covariance analyses had been performed.

CHILDREN'S INTERVIEW MEASURES

The children's responses to the Self-Concept and the Teacher Thinks interviews tended to be predominantly positive—that is, in the direction of the socially desirable response to each item. On the Self-Concept interview, which had 14 items, the range of total positive responses by the children in the matched groups study was 7 to 14, with a median of 13. In the typical groups study, the range of total positive responses was 5 to 14, with a median of 13. Similarly, on the Teacher Thinks interview, the range of the total number of positive responses given by the children in the matched groups study was 7 to 14, with a median of 14; in the typical groups study, the range was 8 to 14 with a median of 13. Because of these skewed distributions, the data were analyzed by partitioned chi-square analyses rather than by analyses of variance. The responses were dichotomized approximately at the median: Children who had never made a negative comment about themselves in the interview (i.e., who had 14 positive responses) were compared with children who had made one or more negative statements about themselves. Although the medians were not exactly equivalent on all sets of data, the same criterion for dichotomizing the responses was used for all sets of data.

Matched Groups Study

An SES × Race × Sex partitioned chi-square analysis of the total number of positive responses to the Self-Concept interview yielded a nonsignificant overall chi-square value. Similar analyses for each of the 14 individual self-concept items also yielded no significant results.

An SES × Race × Sex partitioned chi-square anaysis of the total number of positive responses to the Teacher Thinks interview yielded a nonsignificant overall chi-square value. Similar analyses for each of the 14 items on the Teacher Thinks interview also produced no significant findings.

Relationship Between the Two Interviews. Correlations between children's responses to each of the 14 Self-Concept items and the corresponding item of the Teacher Thinks interview were generally significant, even though they were not large. The median correlation was +.29 ($p < .01$), and the range of correlations was +.13 to +.49.

To further determine the relationship between the child's responses to the two interviews, the child's total number of positive responses to the Teacher Thinks interview was compared with his or her total number of positive responses to the Self-Concept interview. For 43% of the children there was no difference between their overall response to the two interviews, while for the remaining 57% there were deviations of one or more points in the overall scores. On the basis of these responses, a dichotomized difference score ("no difference" versus "a difference of one or more points" in the total number of positive responses) was derived and analyzed by a partitioned SES × Race × Sex chi-square. A significant overall result was obtained. Follow-up analyses revealed that white children were more likely to show a discrepancy in their responses to the two interviews (73% did so) than were black children (42% had discrepant scores), $\chi^2(1) = 9.58, p < .01$. The direction of the discrepancy revealed that white children were likely to report that the teachers' view of them was more positive than their own self-concept, while black children less often reported that their teachers thought highly of them. Of all white children, 56% showed such a difference; only 25% of all black children did so.

Typical Groups Study

An SES × Race × Sex partitioned chi-square analysis of the total number of positive responses to the Self-Concept interview yielded a nonsignificant overall chi-square value. Analyses for each of the 14 items in the Self-Concept interview yielded significant results for 2 items: the questions regarding whether the child liked her or his possessions and whether the child believed he or she was "strong." The significance on the first question was due to a difference between the responses of the two sexes, $X^2(1) = 10.13, p < .01$: Males were more likely than females to state that they did not like their possessions (15% of the males versus 1% of the females). On the question regarding strength, a significant Race × Sex interaction was found, $X^2(1) = 11.58, p < .01$. For females, race made no difference with all but one child reporting herself as "strong." For males, 15% of the white children reported that they were not strong while only 2% of the black children did so.

A partitioned chi-square analysis for the total score on the Teacher Thinks measure yielded a nonsignificant overall chi-square value. Analyses for each of the 14 items in the Teacher Thinks interview yielded one significant finding, on the question of whether or not the child liked his or her possessions. On this question, there was a significant effect for SES, $\chi^2(1) = 5.71, p < .05$, and a significant effect for sex, $\chi^2(1) = 5.71, p < .05$. Advantaged children (94%) compared to disadvantaged children (81%) were more likely to report that they believed their teachers thought that they liked their possessions. Females were more likely than males to report that their teachers thought they liked their possessions (94% versus 81%, respectively).

Relationship Between the Two Interviews. Correlations between the children's responses to each of the 14 Self-Concept interview items and the corresponding items on the Teacher Thinks interview ranged from +.05 to +.45 with a median value of +.27 ($p < .01$).

Comparison of the total scores on the two interviews revealed that 33% of the children had identical scores on the two measures, while the remaining 67% deviated by one or more points in their overall responses to the two interviews. A partitioned chi-square analysis of the dichotomized difference score (see p. 52) yielded a nonsignificant chi-square value.

Relationship Between Interview Responses and Performance

Correlations were calculated between the child's response to each item on the two interviews and his or her scores on each of the 26 performance measures. The principal purpose of this analysis was to determine whether verbal responses to the interview items were related to any actual behavior. Since differences between the matched and typical groups samples were not of particular interest, nor was there any interest in separately examining correlations for different SES, race, or sex groups, the data for all 304 children who served as subjects in any phase of this investigation were pooled and used as the basis for calculating the correlation coefficients. Because of the the high chance of Type I errors that arises when calculating such a large number of correlation coefficients, the criterion was adopted that there be at least two correlations significant at the .01 level or beyond, or that there be at least three correlations at the .05 level, before an interview item would be reported as significantly related to performance. By this criterion, employing a binomial model, the chances of a Type I error are approximately $p < .04$ and $p < .03$, respectively.

Using this criterion of significance, of the 14 items in the Self-Concept interview, responses to three questions were significantly related to performance; of the 14 questions in the Teacher Thinks interview, responses to five questions were significantly related to performance. Table 3.5 presents the correlations that were significant among these questions and the performance measures.

TABLE 3.5

Significant Correlations Between Children's Responses to Interview Questions and Their Performance on Experimental Tasks

(N = 304)

	Self-Concept					Teacher Thinks		
Performance Measure	"Good"	"Like Possessions"	"Happy"	"Talks a Lot"	"Scared of Things"	"Like Posessions"	"Ugly"	"Strong"
Verbal creativity:								
Originality per response	-.12*	-.13*			.20**			
Highest originality	-.13*	-.13*					.15**	
Fluency				.11*		-.16**	.12*	
Flexibility						-.15**		
Dog and Bone:								
Quality per path	-.15**		-.11*					
Highest quality			-.12*				.13*	
Token-in-the-Box:								
Quality per attempt			.13*					
Highest quality								
Five-Objects:								
Highest number			.13*					
Reading:								
First attempt		-.12*			-.12*			
Mean attempt								
Risk								-.15**

Balancing:			
First attempt			
Mean attempt			
Risk	.14*		
Token-in-the-Box:			
Expectancy of success			
Find-the-Surprise:			
First choice			
Total autonomous responses			
Opening Doors:			
Number blank	.12*		
Token-in-the-Box:			
Number of attempts			
Dog and Bone:			
Time to frustration		.12*	
Puzzle:			
Total time			.18**
Walk-the-Board:			
Handholding requests	-.12*		.14*
Puzzle:			
Number of dependency statements	.20**	-.18**	.13*
Five-Objects:			
Requests for feedback			
Needed prompting			-.18**

*$p < .05$.
**$p < .01$.

As can be seen in Table 3.5, children who reported that they were not "good" obtained higher creativity scores on three measures: originality per response and highest originality on the Verbal Creativity tasks, and highest quality path on the Dog and Bone task. Similary, children who reported they did not "like their possessions" had higher Verbal Creativity scores on originality per response and highest originality, and made higher first attempts on the Reading task. Children who reported they were "happy" showed higher creativity on the Token-in-the-Box and the Five-Objects tasks, but children who reported they were not "happy" had higher creativity scores on the Dog and Bone task.

Children who reported that their teachers thought they "talked a lot" showed higher fluency scores on the Verbal Creativity tasks and made more dependency statements on the Puzzle than did children who reported negatively on this interview item. Children who reported their teachers thought they were "scared of things" showed higher originality per response on Verbal Creativity tasks, lower dependency scores on the Walk-the-Board game, higher curiosity on the Opening Doors, greater self-confidence on the Balancing task, but a lower first-level attempt on the Reading task. As compared to other children, those who reported their teachers thought they did not "like their possessions" had higher fluency and flexibility scores on the Verbal Creativity tasks, made more dependency statements on the Puzzle and had a shorter time to their first frustration statement on the Dog and Bone task. Children who reported their teachers thought they were "ugly" showed higher originality and flexibility on the Verbal Creativity tasks, a higher originality per path on the Dog and Bone task, and a lower risk score on the Reading task than did other children. Children who reported their teachers thought they were "strong" made fewer dependency statements and worked longer on the Puzzle, but showed more dependency on the Walk-the-Board game than did children who did not believe their teachers thought they were "strong."

TEACHER RATING SCALE

Matched Groups Study

The 12 items on the teacher rating scale were analyzed by an SES × Race × Sex multivariate analysis of variance, with two levels for each factor and 12 subjects per cell. No significant main effects or interactions were found.

Typical Groups Study

The 12 teacher rating scale items were analyzed by an SES × Race × Sex multivariate analysis of variance with 20 subjects per cell. Significant multivariate main effects were found for SES, $F(12,141) = 3.07, p < .001$, for race, $F(12,141) = 2.76, p < .01$, and for sex, $F(12,141) = 2.36, p < .01$. None of the interactions was significant. Significant univariate F-values for SES were found on six of the 12 rating items: classroom achievement, reading ability, creativity, maturity, persistence, and neatness. In all six cases, the ratings favored the advantaged rather than the disadvantaged children. Significant univariate F-values for race were found on four of the 12 items: independence, curiosity, peer popularity, and neatness. In all four cases, the ratings favored black as compared to white children. Only one of the 12 items, that of maturity, was found to have a significant univariate F-value for sex. Females were rated as significantly more mature than males. The means and significance levels for each of these findings are reported in Table 3.6.

TABLE 3.6
Significant SES, Race, and Sex Effects Found in the Analyses of
Teachers' Ratings in the Typical Groups Study

		Rating			
		Advantaged		Disadvantaged	
Dependent Measure	Univariate F-Value and Probability	$\bar{X}$	SD	$\bar{X}$	SD
SES Effects					
Classroom achievement	$F(1,152) = 4.82, p < .03$	4.34	1.14	3.98	.96
Reading ability	$F(1,152) = 5.91, p < .02$	4.29	1.22	3.85	1.09
Creativity	$F(1,152) = 7.27, p < .01$	4.14	.90	3.74	.99
Maturity	$F(1,152) = 16.42, p < .001$	4.39	1.08	3.70	1.12
Persistence	$F(1,152) = 4.36, p < .04$	4.31	1.34	3.89	1.29
Neatness	$F(1,152) = 27.34, p < .001$	5.02	1.31	4.06	1.11
Race Effects		Black		White	
Independence	$F(1,152) = 6.70, p < .02$	4.45	1.17	4.01	1.05
Curiosity	$F(1,152) = 8.88, p < .01$	4.44	1.00	3.99	.94
Peer popularity	$F(1,152) = 7.83, p < .01$	4.34	.93	3.92	.98
Neatness	$F(1,152) = 6.31, p < .02$	4.78	1.09	4.31	1.42
Sex Effects		Males		Females	
Maturity	$F(1,152) = 3.96, p < .05$	3.88	1.20	4.21	1.09

TABLE 3.7

Summary of Results of Three SES × Race × Sex Multivariate Analyses of Covariance of Teachers' Ratings for the Typical Groups Study[a]

Effect	Multivariate Effects			Measure	Univariate Effects		
	IQ as Covariate	MA as Covariate	IQ & MA as Covariates		IQ as Covariate	MA as Covariate	IQ & MA as Covariates
SES	NS	<.003	NS	Classroom achievement	—	—	—
				Reading ability	—	—	—
				Creativity	—	<.03	—
				Maturity	—	<.01	—
				Persistence	—	—	—
				Neatness	<.001	<.001	<.001
Race	<.001	<.001	<.001	[Classroom achievement]	<.001	<.05	<.001
				[Reading ability]	<.02	—	<.02
				[Maturity]	<.001	<.02	<.001
				Independence	<.001	<.01	<.001
				Curiosity	<.001	<.01	<.001
				[Leadership]	<.03	<.05	<.05
				Peer popularity	<.001	<.01	<.001
				[Persistence]	<.01	<.05	<.01
				Neatness	<.01	<.05	<.01
Sex	<.002	<.007	<.003	Maturity	<.01	<.05	<.01

[a]The nonbracketed measures listed in this table are all of the measures for which significant findings were obtained in the original multivariate analysis of the typical groups data. the bracketed measures attained significance only after the covariance analyses had been performed.

Because of the group differences in MA and IQ, multivariate analyses of covariance were conducted to examine group differences in teachers' ratings with the effects of IQ, MA, and both IQ and MA statistically controlled. Table 3.7 summarizes the results of these three analyses.

As can be seen in Tables 3.6 and 3.7, most SES differences found in the original multivariate analysis were not significant when the two SES groups were statistically equated for IQ. When the groups were statistically equated for MA alone, SES differences in teachers' ratings remained on only half as many items as were found originally. The single significant sex difference revealed in the original analysis, "maturity," was found in all covariance analyses. The original race differences remained significant when the groups were statistically equated for either MA, IQ, or both MA and IQ. In fact, the number of significant univariate F-values for individual rating items increased when the effects of IQ and MA were controlled. On each rating for which significant results were found, teachers rated black children higher than they rated white children.

Relationship Between Teachers' Ratings and Children's Performance

Correlations between each of the teacher-rating-scale items and the children's performance on the 26 dependent measures were calculated for the total sample of 304 children. Using the criterion of significance described in the section on the relationship between children's interview responses and performance (see p. 53), all but two of the 12 teacher-rating-scale items were significantly related to the children's performance scores. However, unlike the children's responses to individual interview items, which were generally intercorrelated to only a small degree, the 12 teacher-rating-scale items were highly intercorrelated. Rather than reporting significant correlations between each of the teacher rating items and the children's performance, therefore, the number of items was reduced to a representative subset of four: "classroom achievement," "fears things," "leadership," and "neatness." The selection of these particular attributes was based upon the results of a principal components factor analysis of the teacher rating items which revealed that four factors were sufficient to account for 75% of the variance. The single item that loaded highest on each of these factors was retained for examination in the present analysis. (Because of the very high loadings of each of the items on a single factor, this procedure was employed rather than using factor scores; under these circum-

TABLE 3.8
Significant Correlations Between Teachers' Ratings and Children's Performance on
Experimental Tasks (N = 304)

Performance Measure	Teacher Ratings			
	Classroom Achievement	Leadership	Neatness	Fearful of Things
Verbal Creativity: Originality per response	.16**			
Verbal Creativity: Highest originality				
Verbal Creativity: Fluency	−.15**		−.20**	
Verbal Creativity: Flexibility			−.12*	
Dog and Bone: Quality per path	.13*	.12*		
Dog and Bone: Highest quality			.15**	
Token-in-the-Box: Quality per attempt				
Token-in-the-Box: Highest quality				
Five-Objects: Highest number	−.11*			
Reading: First attempt	.24**		.14*	−.22**
Reading: Mean attempt	.40**	.16**	.16**	−.35**
Reading: Risk				
Balancing: First attempt		−.12*		
Balancing: Mean attempt				
Balancing: Risk				
Token-in-the-Box: Expectancy of success				
Find-the-Surprise: First choice				
Find-the-Surprise: Total autonomous responses				
Opening Doors: Number blank	.13*		.12*	
Dog and Bone: Time to frustration				.13*
Token-in-the-Box: Number of attempts				
Puzzle: Total time				
Walk-the-Board: Handholding requests	.13*			
Puzzle: Number of dependency statements		.12*	−.14*	
Five-Objects: Requests for feedback				
Five-Objects: Needed prompting				

*p < .05
**p < .01

stances the two procedures yield equivalent findings. The results of the factor analysis are presented in Appendix D.) Table 3.8 presents the correlations that were significant among these four rating items and the performance measures.

As can be seen in Table 3.8, the teachers' rating of classroom achievement was significantly related to approximately one-third of the 26 dependent measures. Children rated "high" on achievement showed greater self-confidence on two of the three Reading-task measures, more curiosity, and higher originality per response on the Verbal Creativity and the Dog and Bone tasks. They also showed greater dependency in the Walk-on-the-Board game, were less fluent on the Verbal Creativity task, and used fewer objects in their performance on the Five-Objects task.

Children rated "high" in leadership showed greater self-confidence on one of the three Reading measures and greater originality per response on the Dog and Bone game than did children rated "low" in leadership. They also showed less self-confidence on one of the three Balancing-task measures and greater dependency on the Puzzle task.

Children rated "high" on neatness evidenced greater self-confidence on two of the three Reading-task measures, were more curious, and were more creative on one of the two Dog and Bone task measures. The neatness rating was negatively related to creativity, as measured by fluency and flexibility on the Verbal Creativity tasks, and to dependency as measured by the number of statements on the Puzzle task.

Children rated as "fearful of things" showed less self-confidence on two of the three Reading-task measures. They also persisted for a longer time on the Dog and Bone game before making a frustration statement than did children who were not judged fearful.

FATHER'S PRESENCE OR ABSENCE

Since all of the advantaged children in the matched groups study and all but six of the advantaged children in the typical groups study came from two-parent families, an analysis of the father's presence or absence factor was not undertaken for the advantaged groups. The disadvantaged children in the matched groups study were selected by design to come half from homes where the family was intact and half from father-absent homes. In the typical groups study, where representative samples were recruited, the incidence of father absence was fortuitously approximately the same as that in the matched groups study. Of the 80 children from disadvantaged families in the typical groups study, 46 (58%) were from father-absent homes. On a cell-by-cell basis across the disadvantaged sample, the percentage of children from father-absent homes was: 60% for black males, 65% for black females; 50% for white males, and 55% for white females. Because of this reasonably balanced cell-size distribution, analyses of the father-absent factor could be conducted in a parallel manner for both studies—that is, with a Race × Sex × Father-absence multivariate analysis of variance for the disadvantaged samples. Preliminary analyses for the typical groups study revealed some significant group differences in MA and IQ; therefore, multivariate analyses of covariance with IQ, MA, and both IQ and MA as covariates were also performed on the data. Finally, since the analyses of the father-absence factor included some re-analyses of previously examined data (e.g., race and sex findings), only significant findings related to father's presence or absence are reported in this section.

Children's Performance Measures

Matched Groups Study. The 23 continuous dependent variables were analyzed by a Race × Sex × Father-absence multivariate analysis of variance with two levels for each factor and 12 subjects per cell. A significant multivariate main effect was found for father-absence, $F(23,66) = 2.17$, $p < .01$. Table 3.9 presents the means and the univariate F-values for the four measures which were found to show a significant univariate main effect for father-absence. (A complete table of the means for each group on each measure is presented in Appendix E.)

As can be seen in Table 3.9, children from father-present homes achieved higher originality-per-response scores and also were more likely to show an overall higher level of originality on the Verbal Creativity tasks than were children from father-absent homes. The latter requested feedback more frequently on the Five-Objects task than did children from father-present homes. On the Balancing task, children from father-absent homes chose significantly harder tasks on their first try than did children from father-present homes.

Race × Sex × Father-absence partitioned chi-square analyses on the three dichotomized variables yielded no significant chi-square values associated with the factor of father-absence.

TABLE 3.9
Significant Father-Absence Effects Found in the Analyses of Children's
Performance in the Matched Groups Study (Disadvantaged Children Only)

Dependent Measure	Univariate F-Value and Probability	Performance			
		Father-Present Children		Father-Absent Children	
		$\bar{X}$	SD	$\bar{X}$	SD
Verbal Creativity:					
Originality per response	$F(1,88) = 5.75, p < .02$	3.02	.71	2.67	.73
Highest originality	$F(1,88) = 5.92, p < .02$	4.34	.83	3.88	.95
Balancing:					
First attempt	$F(1,88) = 5.42, p < .05$	1.64	.79	2.02	.78
Five-Objects:					
Requests for feedback	$F(1,88) = 5.43, p < .05$	4.10	2.92	6.10	5.17

Typical Groups Study. A Race × Sex × Father-absence multi-variate analysis of variance of the 23 continuous variables was performed on the data for the typical groups study. Because of the unequal cell sizes, an unweighted means procedure was employed. No significant effects were obtained involving the father-absence factor. Similarly, no significant findings were obtained in the covariance analyses with MA, IQ, and both MA and IQ covaried. (A complete table of the means for each group on each measure is presented in Appendix F.) Chi-square analyses for father-absence effects on the three dichotomized variables also yielded no significant findings.

Children's Interviews

Matched Groups Study. On both the Self-Concept interview and the Teacher Thinks interviews, chi-square analyses of the total score and of each individual item revealed no significant effects related to father-absence. Similarly the analysis of the difference between the total scores on the two interviews produced no father-absence effects.

Typical Groups Study. A chi-square analysis for the total number of positive responses to the Self-Concept interview yielded a nonsignificant chi-square value. Analyses of responses to each of the 14 interview items yielded a significant father-absence effect for the question regarding whether the child liked other children. Father-absent children were more likely to report not liking other children than were father-present children; 28% of the father-absent compared to 6% of the father-present children reported not liking other children [$\chi^2(1)$ = 6.41, $p < .05$].

An analysis of the total number of positive responses to the Teacher Thinks interview yielded a nonsignificant chi-square value. In the analyses of responses to each of the 14 Teacher Thinks items, one significant effect was found: Father-absent children were more likely than father-present children to report that their teachers did not think they were smart [13% versus 0%, respectively, $\chi^2(1)$ = 4.67, $p < .05$]. An analysis of the difference score between the responses to the two interviews yielded a nonsignificant chi-square value.

Teacher Rating Scale

Matched Groups Study. A Race × Sex × Father-absence multivariate analysis of variance of the teacher-rating-scale items for the economically disadvantaged children in the matched groups study yielded no significant main effects or interactions.

Typical Groups Study. A Race × Sex × Father-absence multivariate analysis of variance of the 12 teacher-rating-scale items yielded a significant multivariate Race × Sex × Father-absence interaction, $F(12,61)$ = 2.24, $p < .02$. Significant univariate F-values for the Race × Sex × Father-absence interaction were found for three items: reading ability, $F(1,72)$ = 5.02, $p < .03$, curiosity, $F(1,72)$ = 7.18, $p < .01$, and persistence, $F(1,72)$ = 4.08, $p < .05$. Table 3.10 presents the means entering into the interaction for each of these three items.

As can be seen in Table 3.10, on each of the three measures, teachers consistently tended to rate father-absent white females and black males lower than their father-present counterparts. Tests for the significance of the father-absence effect for each of the four cells were made by the Newman–Keuls method (Winer, 1971). The difference was significant in only two instances: Father-absent white females were rated significantly lower in curiosity than were father-present white females; and father-absent black males were rated significantly lower in reading ability than were father-present black males. No differences were found

TABLE 3.10

Mean Ratings Entering into the Significant Effects Related to Father-Absence
Obtained in the Analyses of Teachers' Ratings in the Typical Groups Study
(Disadvantaged Children Only)

| | Teacher Rating | | | | | |
| | *Reading Ability* | | *Curiosity* | | *Persistence* | |
Group	*Father Absent*	*Father Present*	*Father Absent*	*Father Present*	*Father Absent*	*Father Present*
Black males	3.42^a	4.50^a	4.33	4.88	3.92	4.75
Black females	4.31	3.86	4.15	3.86	4.15	4.00
White males	3.50	3.50	4.20	3.70	3.90	3.40
White females	3.64	4.22	3.36^a	4.33^a	3.18	4.00

[a]The difference between father-absent and father-present subjects was significant, $p < .05$.

between father-absent and father-present black females and white males.

Re-analyses of the ratings by means of multivariate analyses of covariance with MA, IQ, and both MA and IQ as covariates yielded identical conclusions to those reported for the original analysis.

SCHOOL RACIAL COMPOSITION

Virtually all of the white children in the two studies attended schools that were predominantly white. The effects of school racial composition thus could not be examined for the white children. Only slightly more variation existed for the advantaged black children, all but four of whom attended schools that were at least 50% white in racial composition. Among the disadvantaged black children in both studies, however, a wide range of variation existed in the racial composition of the schools the children attended. In the following analyses, comparisons were made between those disadvantaged black children who attended schools in which at least 50% or more of the children enrolled were black and those disadvantaged black children who attended schools in which 50% or more of the children were white. Since each group had approximately equal numbers of males and females and approximately equal numbers of father-present and father-absent children, the sex and father-absence factors were ignored in the present analyses.

Children's Performance Measures

Matched Groups Study. Whereas 19 children attended predominantly black schools ($\bar{X}$ = 81% black enrollment), 29 children attended predominantly white schools ($\bar{X}$ = 75% white enrollment). The performance of these two groups of children was compared by *t*-tests. Significant values were obtained on five of the 23 continuous dependent measures: the number of requests for feedback on the Five-Objects task, the mean level attempted on the Balancing task, the mean level attempted on the Reading task, the risk score on the Balancing task, and the risk score on the Reading task. Table 3.11 presents the means and the *t*-values for the two groups on these measures. (A complete table of the means and standard deviations for each groups on each measure is presented in Appendix G.)

As can be seen in Table 3.11, disadvantaged black children who attended predominantly black schools showed higher dependency on the Five-Objects measure than did disadvantaged black children who attended predominantly white schools. They also evidenced greater self-confidence on two of the three measures in each of the Reading and Balancing tasks than did the children who attended predominantly white schools. Chi-square analyses of the three dichotomized variables yielded no significant results related to school racial composition.

TABLE 3.11

Mean Values and Significance Levels for Effects Related to School Racial Composition Obtained in Analyses of Children's Performance in the Matched Groups Study (Disadvantaged Black Children Only)

Dependent Measure	t-Value and Probability	Performance			
		Pred. Black School (N = 19)		Pred. White School (N = 29)	
		$\bar{X}$	SD	$\bar{X}$	SD
Reading:					
Mean attempt	$t(46) = 2.16, p < .05$	1.75	.33	1.50	.42
Risk	$t(46) = 2.55, p < .05$	13.10	1.97	10.76	3.59
Balancing:					
Mean attempt	$t(46) = 2.45, p < .05$	1.86	.22	1.68	.25
Risk	$t(46) = 2.19, p < .05$	14.52	2.62	12.69	2.88
Five-Objects:					
Requests for feedback	$t(46) = 2.12, p < .05$	7.47	7.02	4.38	2.58

Typical Groups Study. In the typical groups study, 16 children attended predominantly black schools ($\bar{X}$ = 96% black enrollment) and 24 children attended predominantly white ($\bar{X}$ = 67% white enrollment) schools. The children's performance on the 23 continuous measures was initially compared by *t*-tests. However, it was found that the children who attended predominantly white schools were significantly older when tested than were the children who attended predominantly black schools ($\bar{X}$ = 105 months versus 95 months, respectively, *t*(38) = 4.60, *p* < .001). Since the two groups did not differ significantly on IQ, they consequently differed significantly on MA ($\bar{X}$ = 99 versus 87, respectively, *t*(38) = 3.68, *p* < .001). While several of the *t*-test values comparing the performance of the two groups on the behavioral measures were significant, re-analyses covarying MA eliminated significant differences between the groups. Chi-square analyses of the three dichotomized variables yielded no significant results related to school racial composition.

Children's Interviews

Matched Groups Study. Chi-square analyses were performed comparing the 19 children who attended predominantly black schools with the 29 children who attended predominantly white schools. Results on the total and individual items scores for both the Self-Concept and Teacher Thinks interviews were not significant.

An analysis of the difference score between the total scores on the two interviews produced a significant result, $\chi^2(1)$ = 4.60 (corrected for continuity), *p* < .05. Most of the children (72%) who attended predominantly white schools showed no difference between their Self-Concept score and their Teacher Thinks score, whereas most of the children (72%) who attended predominantly black schools showed a discrepancy between their scores on the two measures. The nature of this discrepancy was that the children who attended predominantly black schools were more likely to report (47% did so) that their teachers overrated them than were the children who attended predominantly white schools (24% of whom made such a report).

Typical Groups Study. None of the chi-square analyses comparing the 16 children who attended predominantly black schools with the 24 children who attended predominantly white schools yielded significant findings. As in the matched groups study, analyses were made on the total response to each of the interviews, the difference between these totals, and each of the 14 items on each of the two interviews.

Teacher Rating Scale

Matched Groups Study. A one-way multivariate analysis of variance, which compared the 19 children who attended predominantly black schools with the 29 children who attended predominantly white schools, was performed on the 12 teacher-rating-scale items. A significant multivariate effect for school racial composition was obtained, $F(12,35) = 2.57, p < .02$. Only one of the 12 rating items, that for "classroom achievement," had a significant univariate main effect for school racial composition, $F(1,46) = 4.63, p < .04$. Children who attended predominantly white schools were rated significantly lower in classroom achievement than were children who attended predominantly black schools ($\bar{X} = 3.7$ and 4.3, respectively).

Typical Groups Study. The 12 rating-scale items were subjected to a one-way multivariate analysis of variance that compared the ratings for the 16 children who attended predominantly black schools with the ratings for the 24 children who attended predominantly white schools. The multivariate effect for school racial composition was not significant. Multivariate analyses of covariance that employed IQ, MA, and both IQ and MA as covariates similarly revealed no effect of school racial composition on the ratings.

STANDARDIZED ACHIEVEMENT TESTS AND OTHER NONEXPERIMENTAL AND BACKGROUND DATA

Findings Related to SES, Ethnic, and Sex Group Membership

The mean values on demographic and standardized test performance variables for each group in both studies are presented in Table 3.12. The tables for the correlations among these variables and the correlations between these variables and the experimental measures can be found in Appendixes H and I.

Matched Groups Study. Significant group differences were found for four of the nine measures shown in Table 3.12: the percentage of white children in the schools attended by the children, the number of siblings, reading achievement, and arithmetic achievement. An SES × Race × Sex analysis of variance on the percentage-of-white-children

TABLE 3.12
Mean Values for Demographic and Standardized Test Measures for the Matched and Typical Samples

SES	Race	Sex	N	Bused (%)	School (% White)	Sibs (#)	Grade (% repeated)	IQ	MA (in yrs.)	CA (in yrs.)	Reading Achievement (grade eq.)	Arithmetic Achievement (grade eq.)
							Matched Groups Study					
Adv.	Bl	F	12	25	72	2.3	0	103	8.8	8.3	4.2	3.4
Adv.	Bl	M	12	33	76	2.6	0	104	8.9	8.4	3.4	3.7
Adv.	Wh	F	12	0	100	4.6	0	100	8.6	8.4	3.9	3.1
Adv.	Wh	M	12	33	100	4.5	0	100	8.7	8.5	3.4	3.2
Disadv.	Bl	F	12	17	47	2.7	0	99	8.6	8.4	2.6	2.5
Disadv.	Bl	M	12	17	54	3.1	0	99	8.6	8.6	2.8	2.5
Disadv.	Wh	F	12	17	97	3.2	0	99	8.7	8.5	3.7	3.5
Disadv.	Wh	M	12	8	98	4.2	0	99	8.4	8.3	3.1	2.8
							Typical Groups Study					
Adv.	Bl	F	20	50	75	2.4	15	102	8.6	8.2	3.5	3.8
Adv.	Bl	M	20	35	82	1.6	10	104	8.7	8.3	3.2	3.3
Adv.	Wh	F	20	0	99	4.0	5	112	9.2	8.0	3.4	3.1
Adv.	Wh	M	20	10	98	3.8	5	117	9.8	8.2	3.9	3.8
Disadv.	Bl	F	20	5	41	3.5	15	89	7.6	8.3	2.6	2.4
Disadv.	Bl	M	20	20	42	3.4	45	93	8.2	8.6	3.0	1.9
Disadv.	Wh	F	20	0	93	3.2	25	102	8.6	8.2	2.8	2.8
Disadv.	Wh	M	20	0	93	3.6	30	105	8.9	8.4	2.8	3.0

measure yielded a significant SES main effect, $F(1,88) = 6.94, p < .01$; a significant race main effect, $F(1,88) = 60.01$, $p < .001$; and a significant SES × Race interaction, $F(1,88) = 5.07, p < .05$. The means entering into the significant interaction were 73.7%, 99.5%, 50.8%, and 97.8% for advantaged black, advantaged white, disadvantaged black, and disadvantaged white children, respectively. Newman–Keuls mean comparisons indicated that disadvantaged black children attended schools that had a significantly lower percentage of white children enrolled than did the remaining three groups. Advantaged black children attended schools with significantly fewer white children in comparison with both advantaged and disadvantaged white children ($p < .01$ for all significant comparisons). An SES × Race × Sex analysis of variance on the number of siblings yielded a significant main effect for race, $F(1,84) = 15.20, p < .001$; black children had an average of 2.7 siblings, whereas white children had an average of 4.1 siblings.

Reading achievement scores were available for 83% of the children in this sample; arithmetic achievement scores were available for 82%. An SES × Race × Sex analysis of variance of the reading achievement scores yielded a significant main effect for SES, $F(1,72) = 10.06$, $p < .01$. The mean grade-equivalence reading score for advantaged children was 3.73, while for disadvantaged children it was 3.06. An analysis of variance of the arithmetic achievement scores yielded a significant main effect for SES, $F(1,71) = 5.69$, $p < .05$, and a significant SES × Race interaction, $F(1,71) = 5.40, p < .05$. The mean grade-equivalence scores of each group were 3.56 for advantaged blacks, 3.14 for advantaged whites, 2.48 for disadvantaged blacks, and 3.13 for disadvantaged whites. Comparisons of these means by the Newman–Keuls method indicated that the disadvantaged black children's achievement was significantly lower than that of the advantaged black children ($p < .05$). The remaining means did not differ significantly.

Typical Groups Study. Significant group differences were found for all of the measures presented in Table 3.12 except CA. A partitioned chi-square analysis of the busing data yielded significant main effects for SES and race, and a significant SES × Race interaction: 42.5% of the black advantaged children were bused to school, a significantly higher percentage than any other group (12.5% of disadvantaged blacks, 5% of advantaged whites, and 0% of disadvantaged whites, all p values $< .01$.)

An SES × Race × Sex analysis of variance on the percentage of white children in the school measure yielded a significant main effect for SES, $F(1,152) = 53.30, p < .001$; a significant main effect for race, $F(1,152) = 157.49, p < .001$; and a significant SES × Race interaction, $F(1,152) = 28.85, p < .001$. The means entering into the significant interaction were 78.2%, 98.8%, 41.7%, and 93.2% for advantaged black, advantaged white, disadvantaged black, and disadvantaged white children, respectively. Newman–Keuls comparisons of the means indicated that disadvantaged black children compared to all other groups attended schools that had a significantly lower percentage of white children enrolled. Further, advantaged black children, compared to both classes of white children, attended schools with significantly fewer white children enrolled ($p < .01$ for each significant comparison).

An SES × Race × Sex analysis of the number of siblings yielded a significant main effect for race, $F(1,152) = 8.86$, $p < .01$, and a significant SES × Race interaction, $F(1,152) = 10.31$, $p < .01$. The means entering into the significant interaction were 2.0, 3.9, 3.4, and 3.4 for advantaged blacks, advantaged whites, disadvantaged blacks, and disadvantaged whites, respectively. Comparison of the means by the Newman–Keuls method showed that the advantaged black children had significantly fewer siblings than did all other groups of children ($p < .05$).

A partitioned chi-square analysis of the school retention variable revealed that disadvantaged children were significantly more likely to have repeated a grade than were advantaged children [29% versus 9%, respectively, $\chi^2(1) = 9.24$, $p < .01$]. An SES × Race × Sex analysis of variance of IQ scores yielded a significant main effect for SES, $F(1,152) = 43.39$, $p < .001$; and for race, $F(1,152) = 51.67$, $p < .001$. The mean IQ scores for advantaged and disadvantaged children, respectively, were 109.0 and 97.8; the mean IQ scores for black and white children were 97.3 and 109.6, respectively. An SES × Race × Sex analysis of variance of MA scores yielded significant main effects for SES, $F(1,152) = 20.30$, $p < .001$; for race, $F(1,152) = 28.00, p < .001$; and for sex, $F(1,152) = 5.45$, $p < .05$. The mean MA scores for advantaged and disadvantaged children, respectively, were 108.9 and 100.0; for black and white children, the mean MA scores were 99.2 and 109.7, respectively; and the mean MA score for males was 106.8, for females, 102.2.

Reading achievement scores were available for 90% of the children in the sample; arithmetic achievement scores were available for 77%. An

SES × Race × Sex analysis of variance of the reading achievement scores yielded a significant main effect for SES, $F(1,136) = 20.06$, $p < .001$. The mean grade-equivalence reading score for advantaged children was 3.51, whereas for disadvantaged children it was 2.81. An analysis of variance of the arithmetic achievement scores yielded a significant main effect for SES, $F(1,115) = 29.46$, $p < .001$; a significant SES × Race interaction, $F(1,115) = 5.36$, $p < .05$; and a significant Race × Sex interaction, $F(1,115) = 6.05$, $p < .05$. The means entering into the SES × Race interaction were 3.59, 3.46, 2.19, and 2.90 for the advantaged blacks, advantaged whites, disadvantaged blacks, and disadvantaged whites, respectively. Comparisons of the four means by the Newman–Keuls method revealed that the disadvantaged black children had significantly lower arithmetic achievement scores than did all other groups of children ($p < .01$), and that the disadvantaged white children had significantly lower scores than did the two advantaged groups ($p < .05$). The Race × Sex interaction means were 3.10 for black females, 2.68 for black males, 2.94 for white females, and 3.42 for white males. Comparisons of the means by the Newman–Keuls method indicated that the black males had significantly lower arithmetic achievement scores than did the white males ($p < .05$). None of the remaining differences among the means was significant.

Because of group differences in MA and IQ, the achievement data were re-analyzed with analyses of covariance with MA, IQ, and both MA and IQ as covariates. The results of these analyses yielded a pattern of findings equivalent to those just reported with one exception: The SES × Race interaction for arithmetic achievement scores was not significant when MA was covaried.

Findings Related to Father's Presence or Absence

The mean values on demographic and standardized test performance measures for the father-present and the father-absent disadvantaged children in the matched and typical groups samples are presented in Table 3.13.

Matched Groups Study. A Race × Sex × Father-absence analysis of variance of the number of siblings yielded a significant Race × Father-absence interaction, $F(1,84) = 12.08$, $p < .001$. The means entering into this interaction were 2.90, 3.71, 4.08, and 2.25 for black father-present, white father-present, black father-absent, and white father-absent children, respectively. Comparison of the means by the

TABLE 3.13
Mean Values for Demographic and Standardized Test Measures for
Father-Absent and Father-Present Children (Disadvantaged Children Only)

Race	Sex	Father Pr/AB	N	Bused (%)	School (% White)	Sibs (#)	Grade (% repeated)	IQ	MA (in yrs.)	CA (in yrs.)	Reading Achievement (grade eq.)	Arithmetic Achievement (grade eq.)
							Matched Groups Study					
Bl	F	Pr	12	17	47	2.7	0	99	8.6	8.4	2.6	2.5
Bl	F	Ab	12	17	42	3.9	0	101	8.8	8.5	3.3	3.1
Bl	M	Pr	12	17	54	3.1	0	99	8.6	8.6	2.8	2.5
Bl	M	Ab	12	33	68	4.2	0	98	8.6	8.5	2.7	3.0
Wh	F	Pr	12	17	97	3.2	0	99	8.7	8.5	3.7	3.5
Wh	F	Ab	12	25	91	2.5	0	98	8.4	8.4	3.5	3.3
Wh	M	Pr	12	8	98	4.2	0	99	8.4	8.3	3.1	2.8
Wh	M	Ab	12	0	92	2.0	0	100	8.7	8.4	3.1	3.1
							Typical Groups Study					
Bl	F	Pr	7	0	40	3.4	29	92	7.9	8.3	2.7	2.4
Bl	F	Ab	13	8	41	3.5	8	88	7.5	8.3	2.6	2.4
Bl	M	Pr	8	12	40	3.6	50	92	8.1	8.6	3.2	2.0
Bl	M	Ab	12	25	44	3.2	42	93	8.2	8.6	2.8	1.9
Wh	F	Pr	9	0	94	3.1	11	105	8.8	8.2	2.9	2.7
Wh	F	Ab	11	0	93	3.3	36	100	8.5	8.3	2.7	2.9
Wh	M	Pr	10	0	95	2.9	30	108	9.2	8.4	2.7	3.0
Wh	M	Ab	10	0	91	4.2	30	102	8.6	8.3	2.9	3.0

Newman–Keuls method revealed the white father-absent and the black father-absent children differed significantly ($p < .05$). No other significant father-absence effects were found.

Typical Groups Study. No significant effects involving the father-absence factor were found in any analyses.

Findings Related to the Racial Composition of the Schools

The mean values on demographic and standardized test performance variables for each of the disadvantaged black samples studied in the previous section on school racial composition are presented in Table 3.14.

Matched Groups Study. As might be expected, the percentage of children bused to school was significantly higher for those children who attended predominantly white schools compared to those who attended predominantly black schools ($p = .003$ by Fisher's Exact Test). For the schools defined in this study as "predominantly black," the average number of white children in attendance was 19%; in the "predominantly white" schools, the average was 75%, $t(46) = 12.32$, $p < .001$. Reading achievement data were available for 16 of the 19 disadvantaged black children who attended predominantly black schools, and for 23 of the 29 disadvantaged black children who attended predominantly white schools. Arithmetic achievement data were available for 17 and 22 of the children in these two groups, respectively. Comparisons of the means of the two groups by t-tests yielded no significant findings for either reading or arithmetic achievement scores.

Typical Groups Study. For the schools defined in this study as "predominantly black," the average number of white children in attendance was 4%; in the "predominantly white" schools, the average was 67% [$t(38) = 21.56$, $p < .001$]. The two samples differed significantly in CA and MA: The children who attended the predominantly white schools were significantly older, $t(38) = 4.60$, $p < .001$, and had significantly higher MAs, $t(38) = 3.68$, $p < .001$, than children who attended predominantly black schools.

Reading achievement data were available for 13 of the 16 disadvantaged black children who attended predominantly black schools and for 23 of the 24 disadvantaged black children who attended

TABLE 3.14

Mean Values for Demographic and Standardized Test Measures for Children Who Attended Predominantly Black and Predominantly White Schools (Disadvantaged Black Children Only)

Type of School Attended	N	Bused (%)	School (% White)	Sibs (#)	Grade (% repeated)	IQ	MA (in yrs.)	CA (in yrs.)	Reading Achievement (grade eq.)	Arithmetic Achievement (grade eq.)
Matched Groups Study										
Predominantly black	19	0	19	3.8	0	101	8.7	8.5	2.7	2.8
Predominantly white	29	34	75	3.3	0	99	8.6	8.5	3.0	2.0
Typical Groups Study										
Predominantly black	16	0	4	3.6	31	91	7.3	7.9	2.0	1.7
Predominantly white	24	21	67	3.4	29	92	8.3	8.8	3.3	2.9

predominantly white schools. Arithmetic achievement data were available for 13 and 9 children in these two groups, respectively. The mean reading achievement scores of the two groups differed significantly, $t(34) = 4.31$, $p < .001$, as did the mean arithmetic achievement scores, $t(20) = 5.24$, $p < .001$. In each case, the children who attended predominantly white schools had higher achievement scores than the children who attended predominantly black schools.

As indicated earlier, while these two groups did not differ on IQ, they did differ significantly on CA, and thus on MA. An analysis of covariance employing MA as the covariate was therefore conducted on the achievement data. The results of these analyses were equivalent to those just reported. That is, even with the effects of MA statistically controlled, the children who attended predominantly white schools had higher achievement scores than did the children who attended predominantly black schools.

Comparison of the Samples in the Matched and Typical Studies

A comparison of the 96 matched groups study children with the 160 typical groups study children was made by a Study (Matched versus Typical) × SES × Race × Sex analysis of variance on the variables of IQ, MA, CA, number of siblings, and percentage of white children in the schools attended by the subjects. A comparable partitioned chi-square analysis was conducted to compare the studies on percentage of children bused to school. Significant differences between the two studies were found only for IQ and MA.

For IQ, the main effect for study was significant, $F(1,240) = 4.52$, $p < .05$, and there were significant interactions for Study × SES, $F(1,240) = 11.58$, $p < .001$, and for Study × Race, $F(1,240) = 31.20$, $p < .001$. The means entering into the Study × SES interaction were 102.1, 109.0, 99.4, and 97.8 for matched advantaged, typical advantaged matched disadvantaged, and typical disadvantaged children, respectively. Comparison of the means by the Newman–Keuls method revealed that the advantaged children in the matched groups study had significantly lower IQs than the typical groups study advantaged children ($p < .05$), while the disadvantaged children in the two studies did not differ significantly. The Study × Race interaction means were 101.6 for the matched black children, 97.3 for the typical black children, 99.9 for the matched white children, and 109.6 for the typical white children. Newman–Keuls mean comparisons revealed that white children in the matched groups study had significantly lower IQs than did the typical groups study white children. The black children in the two studies did not differ significantly.

The analysis for MA yielded a significant Study × SES interaction, $F(1,240) = 4.96$, $p < .05$, and a significant Study × Race interaction, $F(1,240) = 14.68$, $p < .001$. The means entering into the Study × SES interaction were 105.1, 108.9, 103.0, and 100.0 for matched advantaged, typical advantaged, matched disadvantaged, and typical disadvantaged children respectively. Newman–Keuls comparisons showed that only the means for the disadvantaged compared to the advantaged typical groups differed significantly ($p < .05$); neither the advantaged nor the disadvantaged matched groups differed significantly in MA from their typical groups counterparts. The Study × Race interaction means were 104.7 for the matched black children, 99.2 for the typical black children, 103.4 for the matched white children, and 109.7 for the typical white children. Newman–Keuls mean comparisons revealed that only the black compared to the white children in the typical groups study differed significantly ($p < .05$); neither the black nor the white matched groups children differed significantly in MA from their typical groups counterparts.

Comparisons of the disadvantaged samples in both studies were also made in order to determine whether the father-absent and father-present subgroups in the matched groups study differed from their typical groups counterparts. Only one significant effect involving father absence was found: a significant Study × Race × Father-absence interaction for the number of siblings, $F(1,156) = 32.05$, $p < .01$. Further examination of this effect revealed, however, that it did not reflect the existence of any significant difference between comparable subgroups of the matched versus typical groups studies. Rather, it indicated that in the matched groups study, father-absent black children had significantly more siblings than did father-absent white children ($p < .05$), whereas this difference was not significant in the typical groups study.

Comparisons of Early- and Late-Tested Children

The testing period for each of the two studies spanned approximately eight months. The data were therefore analyzed to determine whether systematic time-related sources of error (e.g., examiner fatigue, examiner practice effects) might have influenced the findings. In the matched groups study, the earliest-tested child in each cell was selected to form a sample of 12 children who were compared with a sample of 12 children comprised of the latest-tested child in each cell. Comparisons of these groups by *t*-tests showed no significant differences between them on any experimental measure. For the typical groups study, the two earliest-tested children and the two latest-tested children in each cell were chosen to form two samples of 16 children each. Comparisons of these samples by *t*-tests again showed no significant differences between them on any experimental measures.

4 Discussion

The single most important finding in the present investigation was that no one group of children showed uniformly superior or inferior performance across the wide variety of tasks employed in these studies; rather, different stylistic patterns of performance were revealed. A second general finding was that ethnicity was much less predictive of behavior than was social class. The outcome of the present investigation also has implications for the optimal sampling procedure and design of studies directed toward the investigation of SES and ethnic-group differences in behavior. We will discuss these methodological implications before turning to the substantive findings of the two studies.

METHODOLOGICAL CONSIDERATIONS

SES Differences

When two populations differ on some important variable, it has been a common practice to try to control for the difference by using matching procedures. Although a number of objections have been leveled against the use of matching as a means of increasing precision in experimentation (reviewed by Chen, 1967), the most frequent argument against matching is that the procedure is likely to result in samples which are atypical of the populations to which the researcher wishes to generalize (Campbell & Erlebacher, 1970; Campbell & Stanley, 1966; Meehl, 1970). A comparison of the matched and typical groups studies in the present investigation provides some support for this argument.

The very small number of significant SES differences obtained in the matched groups study appears to be due to comparing samples of children that were nonrepresentative of the total population from which they were drawn. In the matched groups design it is assumed that one is comparing a sample of relatively high-IQ economically disadvantaged children with a sample of relatively low-IQ economically advantaged children. The data from the present investigation are partially consistent with this assumption. The advantaged children in the two studies were clearly very different from each other: advantaged children in the matched groups study were, in fact, nearly a full standard deviation lower in IQ than were advantaged children in the typical groups study. Their performance on many tasks may therefore have been affected by the fact that relative to their own reference group they have probably experienced considerable failure. While the disadvantaged samples in the two studies did not differ significantly in IQ and MA, matching may also have produced a somewhat atypical disadvantaged sample. Almost one-third of the typical disadvantaged children had repeated a grade in school, for example, whereas none of the matched samples children had experienced school failure. Such a difference in life experiences may well have had a number of important consequences, even if no differences were evident in the children's standardized test performance.

As Zigler and Child have noted (1973), SES differences found in studies that do not control for developmental level also raise problems of interpretation. Are the differences due to social class membership per se, or are they related to the fact that the disadvantaged children are generally at a lower developmental level than the advantaged children, as defined by MA and/or IQ? This interpretive problem was approached in the typical groups study through the use of covariance analyses in which both MA and IQ were employed as covariates. (Since the children in this study varied somewhat on chronological age, covarying both MA and IQ constituted the most conservative procedure).[1] The similarity in findings of SES differences before and after the covariance indicates that these differences in behavior were related to SES rather than to differences in developmental level. These findings further indicate that those differences reported in studies

---

[1]Among subjects varying in chronological age, MA is the most defensible measure of developmental level. Among subjects all of the same age, however, IQ and MA are perfectly correlated and either IQ or MA can be employed as the measure of developmental level.

investigating SES differences in behavior which did not covary IQ and MA may be more reliable than the criticisms of Zigler and Child (1973) would suggest. It nonetheless appears that the most conservative design for testing for SES differences in behavior is a design employing a covariance analysis in which MA and IQ are the covariates.

In summary, far fewer significant SES differences were obtained in the matched groups study than in the typical groups study. Had the matched groups study not been followed by the typical groups study, the erroneous interpretation could have been advanced that if the developmental level of two SES groups were controlled by matching there would be very few SES differences in behavior. The typical groups study not only resulted in many more significant SES differences, but also resulted in findings much more consistent with those reported in earlier literature.

Ethnic-Group Differences

The methodological implications for the ethnicity variable are quite different from those discovered for the SES variable. The two significant ethnic-group findings (out of 26) in the typical groups study failed to maintain significance when the effects of IQ and MA were covaried. It thus appears that differences between black and white children obtained in the typical groups study were due to differences in IQ and MA existing between the groups, rather than to ethnic group membership per se. The importance of the MA and IQ variables can also be seen in the matched groups study, where no effects of ethnicity were obtained. One can only wonder how many previously reported differences in behavior which have been attributed to ethnic group membership have been obtained because of a failure to control for ethnic group differences in MA and/or IQ.

The methodological implications of the present investigation for research on ethnic group differences are clear: No behavioral differences between ethnic groups on any performance measure should be attributed to ethnicity until the investigator has controlled for the effects of IQ and MA. The empirical findings of the present study suggest that reliable findings concerning group differences require more stringent control procedures when studying ethnic differences than when studying SES differences. Complicating this matter further is the fact that in our society ethnicity and social class are related. It is unfortunately a common practice to compare the performance of advantaged whites to disadvantaged blacks and to interpret any differences as being due to ethnic group membership. In studies of this sort, the differences are uninterpretable unless the design makes it possible to assess or control for SES effects independently of ethnic group effects. In regard to both the SES and ethnic group variables, the conservative strategy would appear to be always to control statistically for MA and IQ through a covariance procedure.

THE ADEQUACY OF CONSTRUCT ASSESSMENT

The desirable criteria for trait measurement—relative independence from measures of other traits and consistency across different measures of the same trait—were met more adequately for some of the six traits under investigation than for others. Two of the hypothesized traits, creativity and self-confidence, appeared well-gauged by measures which correlated significantly across different methods of assessing the traits and which were reasonably independent of measures of other traits. In addition, it was clear that the quality and quantity aspects of creativity were differentiable. Frustration threshold and dependency similarly met the criterion of being manifested across more than one measure, but they were not independent of one another. The curiosity measure was related to measures of several other traits and to mental age. The autonomy measure met the desired criterion of independence from measures of other traits, but conclusions based upon this measure would have been strengthened had more than one task been employed to assess autonomy. We would therefore judge the trait measurement in this investigation as good for creativity and self-confidence, adequate for frustration threshold and dependency, and weak for curiosity and autonomy.

Creativity

Measures to assess creativity were obtained on five tasks: Product Improvement and Unusual Uses (the Verbal Creativity tasks), Dog and Bone, Token-in-the-Box, and Five-Objects. Measures on all but the Five-Objects task were found to be sufficiently interrelated to suggest that they were tapping a dimension of behavior in common. The failure of the Five-Objects measure to be significantly related to measures on the other four tasks may have been due to the fact that the range of responses was restricted by the design of the task.

Creativity has not usually been considered a unitary phenomenon. As previously described, in creativity research it has been customary to distinguish the quantity of ideas which a person can generate (fluency) from the quality of the creative output (originality), and from the tendency to spontaneously shift sets (flexibility). Consistent with previous research (Guilford et al., 1951; Torrance, 1965; Yamamoto & Chimbidis, 1966), in the present investigation these three aspects of creativity were positively related. Highly fluent children tended to produce a higher overall level of original ideas and also to show greater flexibility in their thought. In the present investigation, however, the originality scores were purposely made independent of the fluency score.

Originality, independent of fluency, was found to show consistency across several tasks. Originality scores on the two verbal tasks (Product Improvement and Unusual Uses) were, in fact, so highly correlated that scores were collapsed across the tasks in order to reduce redundancy in the statistical analyses. Verbal originality, in turn, was positively related to originality on the Dog and Bone and the Token-in-the-Box games, both of which were nonverbal tasks.

The originality measures were generally positively related to measures of self-confidence, curiosity, and independence (e.g., highly original children made fewer requests for assistance on the Walk-the-Board and Puzzle tasks). The relationships among the originality and frustration threshold measures were mixed, but high originality was generally associated with greater persistence on frustrating tasks (Puzzle, Dog and Bone, and Token-in-the-Box).

The fluency and flexibility aspects of creativity seemed to reflect an overall verbal responsiveness during testing. For example, highly fluent children were quick to make a statement of frustration during the Dog and Bone task and made more requests for help on the Puzzle task. The negative relationship between the fluency and flexibility measures and the curiosity measure is somewhat puzzling, but perhaps can be explained by the fact that the curiosity task was essentially nonverbal, or in terms of the relationship of these variables to mental age.

Self-Confidence

Measures to assess self-confidence were obtained on three tasks, Reading, Balancing, and the Token-in-the-Box. The Reading task and Balancing task measures were substantially intercorrelated, providing evidence of a general trait of self-confidence in both academic and nonacademic problem situations. The third task measure, intended to assess a child's confidence in his or her ability to succeed on the Token-in-the-Box, was unrelated to the other self-confidence measures. It was, however, highly related to the number of attempts the child made to remove the token from the box. At least for this specific task, then, there appears to be some evidence that a child's stated confidence in his or her abilities was related to the amount of effort the child actually exerted in working on a frustrating task. One could further assume that a willingness to risk failure was a factor in creativity: as noted before, the self-confidence and creativity measures were positively related. The self-confidence measures were also generally positively related to the curiosity and autonomy measures.

Autonomy

Measures to assess autonomy were obtained from a single task, the Find-the-Surprise game. Despite the positive relationship between the autonomy measures and the self-confidence indices, the autonomy measures can best be characterized by their overall independence from most of the remaining measures in this investigation. If it can be argued that the Find-the-Surprise game has face validity as a measure of a child's autonomy, then such autonomy appears to be separate from the other traits assessed.

Curiosity

Curiosity was quite another matter. As Kreitler et al. (1975) have pointed out, efforts to measure curiosity have frequently foundered on the problem of definition. A number of tasks, each with high face validity as measures of curiosity, may show virtually no intercorrelations. The present investigation suggests that independence between traits may also be problematic when measuring curiosity. The Opening Doors task appears to have measured to some degree at least two of the six traits under investigation. (Since this measure did not differentiate among groups when effects of MA differences were controlled, the problems of interpretation which would have arisen can fortunately be sidestepped.) In future investigations it is clear that multiple measures of curiosity should be employed and that the relationships of these measures to other trait measures should be explored in order to determine whether curiosity can be considered a trait independent from the other traits under study.

Frustration Threshold

The three tasks (Puzzle, Dog and Bone, and Token-in-the-Box) employed to assess children's frustration threshold were sufficiently interrelated to suggest that all were measuring a dimension of behavior in common. For example, children who spent a long time trying to solve the Puzzle task also made more attempts to remove the token from the box, and they presisted on the Dog and Bone task for a longer time before verbally expressing any frustration.

One measure of frustration threshold—the time to a frustration statement on the Dog and Bone task—was related to two of the dependency measures. There was also a slight relationship between frustration threshold and creativity, as previously mentioned.

Dependency

Of the four measures designed to assess dependency, three were significantly correlated: the number of dependency statements made while working on the Puzzle, the number of requests for feedback on the Five-Objects task, and whether the child needed prompting to give a solution to the Five-Objects problem. The fourth measure, hand-holding on the Walk-the-Board task, was independent of almost all other behavioral measures in the study.

There is some evidence in these findings for a general trait of verbal dependency. Perhaps not surprisingly, this verbal dependency cannot be separated from verbally expressed frustration (on the Dog and Bone frustration measure). In the present investigation, the attempt to fully separate frustration threshold from dependency may have failed because the two traits in fact are not entirely independent. The present results suggest that a better distinction might have been between persistence and verbal dependency. Children's behavioral persistence in trying to solve difficult problems was consistent across different tasks but was unrelated to their verbal-dependency statements. There is also evidence in the present findings that a trait of "dependency" may not generalize across both physical and intellectual tasks.

CHILDREN'S PERFORMANCE MEASURES

SES Differences

Significant SES differences were obtained on measures of four of the six constructs investigated: creativity, self-confidence, dependency, and curiosity. No differences were found on the autonomy or frustration threshold measures. The significant SES findings on the measures of these constructs were as follows.

Creativity. SES differences in creativity were obtained on five of the nine measures of creativity: originality per response, total fluency, and total flexibility on the Verbal Creativity tasks; quality per path on the Dog and Bone task; and the highest quality attempt on the Token-in-the-Box task. The first four differences were revealed in the typical groups study, with all but the Dog and Bone measure continuing to be significant after the covariance procedures. The last measure was found to differentiate the SES groups in the matched study.

In general, the children in one social-class group were not found to be consistently more creative than children in the other social-class group, and, as predicted, different patterns of performance emerged for each group. The disadvantaged children performed best on those measures of creativity which depended primarily upon the sheer number of responses emitted (i.e., the Verbal Creativity measures of fluency and flexibility). The advantaged children, on the other hand, obtained higher scores on those measures which assessed the quality of each response. The pattern of findings on the creativity measures suggests that the disadvantaged children are more adventuresome and are willing to give a large number of responses without being particularly concerned about the quality of the response given. The advantaged children seem to respond to the creativity tasks in a more constricted manner, perhaps censoring out those responses that do not meet some internalized standard of acceptability. This pattern of findings appears to be generally consistent with earlier findings that have reported greater creativity and spontaneity in disadvantaged as compared with advantaged children (Alper, Blane, & Abrams, 1955; Rogers, 1968).

The better performance of advantaged children on the quality measures, however, raises the issue of whether these higher scores reflect a lower capacity for high-level creative responses on the part of the disadvantaged children or reflect no more than a stylistic performance phenomenon. That is, disadvantaged children may be less inhibited or less fearful of failure and therefore more willing to give a relatively large number of low-quality responses. The pattern of findings appears to favor the stylistic explanation. If the higher quality scores of the advantaged children were reflecting a difference in the capacity for the production of high-quality creativity responses, then we would also expect the advantaged children to perform better than disadvantaged children on the highest originality score for the Verbal Creativity tasks, on the highest quality path for the Dog and Bone task, on the highest quality attempt on the Token-in-the-Box task, and on the highest number of objects used in the Five-Objects task. In fact, with one exception in the matched groups study, no significant differences between the two SES groups were found on these four measures, indicating that the disadvantaged children were just as capable as the advantaged children of producing high-quality responses. Rather, the advantaged children tended to limit their responses to high-quality responses, whereas the disadvantaged children produced their high-quality responses in combination with lower quality responses. Thus there appears to be a response bias operating rather than a real difference in creative ability.

One possible interpretation of the stylistic difference in creativity is that disadvantaged children were more impulsive, and simply failed to inhibit the production of low-level responses. While a number of other studies (reviewed by Messer, 1976) have found disadvantaged children to be more impulsive than advantaged children, in the present study this interpretation does not seem justified. No differences, for example, were found between the SES groups on any measure of frustration threshold, indicating that disadvantaged children did not "impulsively" terminate their performance on a variety of complex tasks.

The present findings seem more related to the results of a study by Hersch (1962), who assessed the creativity of responses to Rorschach stimuli. Hersch's findings indicated that it was a pattern of producing both high- and low-level responses in close association that most characterized the creative adult. That is, high creativity was not associated with a tendency to give consistently high-level responses but rather with a free and spontaneous mingling of ideas of both higher and lower developmental levels.

The present findings also have educational implications. The consequences of children's stylistic differences in the educational environment have been examined by Hertzig et al. (1968) in a study of middle-class white and working-class Puerto Rican children. Hertzig and her colleagues found that even when IQ was controlled, the two groups responded differently to cognitive demands. These investigators suggested that the behavioral style of the Puerto Rican children could easily lead teachers to infer that these children were unmotivated, immature, and lacking in educational potential. Similarly, the stylistic differences found between the SES groups in the present investigation might be so misinterpreted. The child who gives both "right" and "wrong" answers when called upon in the classroom may well be considered less capable than the child who gives only "right" answers. If this is the case, how can educators respond to such children in a more productive fashion? Hertzig and her colleagues suggest that, rather than judging one style as superior and attempting to modify the style that does not fit the classroom, more attention should be given to "introducing greater versatility in teaching" and to finding "modes of instruction and conditions for learning that are optimal for the group of children being taught" [p. 50]. The stylistic differences found in the present investigation may provide some clues for formulating optimal methods of instruction for disadvantaged children.

Self-Confidence. The two SES groups differed on four of the seven self-confidence measures, and, as predicted, the direction of the group differences depended upon the type of task. In general, advantaged children showed greater self-confidence on the Reading task, whereas disadvantaged children showed greater self-confidence on the Balancing task. Advantaged children from both the matched and typical groups studies chose harder problems both on their first attempt and across all attempts on the Reading task, findings which remained significant after covariance analyses. The greater self-confidence of advantaged children on the Reading task is not surprising in light of the repeated findings that advantaged children are more proficient in reading than disadvantaged children. What is surprising was the consistency of this self-confidence difference even when MA and IQ were controlled. Indeed, it is striking that even the most capable disadvantaged children showed such low expectations in their abilities. It would be informative to determine whether, for disadvantaged children, the present findings would generalize to other academic tasks as well as Reading.

The finding that disadvantaged children attempted harder problems on the first trial of the Balancing task has several possible interpretations. One could infer that disadvantaged children are motorically more capable than advantaged children. Since the finding was obtained only in the typical groups study and only on the first attempt (not the mean), another interpretation seems more likely. The motor ability and coordination involved in the Balancing task may be more highly valued by disadvantaged than advantaged children. If this is the case, disadvantaged children may be more familiar with games of physical skill and consequently more confident of their abilities to succeed on them. The advantaged children, on the other hand, appeared to respond somewhat cautiously to the Balancing task as well as to several other unfamiliar tasks in the investigation. While the advantaged children had probably experienced considerable success reading, and were therefore willing to risk harder levels on the Reading task, they were seemingly unfamiliar with what they might encounter on the Balancing task and therefore approached it cautiously. Once they had ascertained the actual difficulty level of the task, however, they were willing to risk as much as were disadvantaged children.

Dependency. SES differences were found on three of the four measures of dependency. Again the findings were not unidirectional. On the Puzzle task, disadvantaged children in both the matched and typical groups studies made more dependency statements than advantaged children. On the Five-Objects task, disadvantaged children in the typical groups study were also more likely to ask for feedback in the face of failure, whereas advantaged children needed to be prompted to do so. It appears that when confronted with a difficult task, disadvantaged children are more likely to ask for help than are advantaged children. Two interpretations of this finding can be given. Advantaged children may be more stringently socialized towards independence than are disadvantaged children, and/or, confronted with a difficult academic task, the disadvantaged children feel less confident of their abilities and therefore are more willing to ask for assistance.

The first explanation seems more likely for several reasons. Despite the difficulty of the task, disadvantaged children in fact persisted as long as advantaged children persisted in trying to solve the Puzzle. This fact indicates that the disadvantaged children had as much (or as little) confidence in their ability eventually to solve the task but that they were more willing verbally to express their doubts and ask for help. The advantaged children's behavior on the Five-Objects task suggests an extreme reluctance to risk humiliation by venturing a solution in which they could have no confidence. The Five-Objects task was deliberately ambiguous, having no obvious or satisfying solution. Given this ambiguity and the belief that some correct solution must exist, advantaged children appeared unwilling to admit to their failure to find the solution without assitance. That we are dealing here with a phenomenon particularly evoked in the face of academic tasks rather than a generalized tendency toward dependence or independence is suggested by the failure of the two SES groups to differ in their dependency behaviors on the Walk-the-Board task. Further, no differences were found between the groups on the autonomy measures.

Curiosity. In the typical groups study, advantaged children were found to show more curiosity than disadvantaged children on the Opening Doors task. This significant SES effect was not found in the covariance analyses, nor was it found in the matched groups study. It appears that if one controls for developmental level, either statistically or with a matched groups design, no evidence is forthcoming that the two SES groups differ in regard to curiosity. The indication that curiosity as measured by the Opening Doors task is positively related to MA and/or IQ level is consistent with the findings of earlier studies (Harter & Zigler, 1974). In light of the evidence that curiosity is not a unitary trait (Kreitler et al., 1975), future studies investigating the relationship between SES and curiosity should employ a number of curiosity measures, rather than the single measure employed in the present investigation.

General Comments on the SES Findings. At this point a brief overview would give perspective to the scope and pattern of the SES differences that were obtained. Across both studies, differences in performance between advantaged and disadvantaged children were found on tasks measuring curiosity, creativity, self-confidence, and dependency. With the exception of curiosity, different patterns of performance emerged for each group on each of the traits investigated. In general, these findings were specific to the typical groups study. Only one finding, the highest quality attempt on the Token-in-the-Box task, was specific to the matched groups study; three findings, the first and mean attempts on the Reading task and the number of dependency statements on the Puzzle task, were consistent across studies.

On the Creativity tasks, advantaged children performed better on the Dog and Bone quality-per-path, the Token-in-the-Box highest quality attempt, and the Verbal originality-per-response measures; whereas the disadvantaged children performed better on the Verbal fluency and flexibility measures. Both groups of children demonstrated self-confidence in their performance; however, advantaged children showed more self-confidence on the first and across all attempts on the Reading task, and disadvantaged children showed more self-confidence on the first attempt on the Balancing task. The dependency tasks also revealed that the children expressed their need for help differently: Disadvantaged children verbally requested help on the Five-Objects and Puzzle tasks, whereas advantaged children needed to be prompted to give a solution to the Five-Objects task. On the basis of these findings, two rather different styles of performance can be said to characterize each group of children. The academically competent advantaged children exhibited curiosity and self-confidence in their approach to academic tasks, and were concerned with the quality of their responses to all tasks presented them. The disadvantaged children were spontaneous and flexible in their approach to problems, showed confidence in their motoric ability, and were able to continue task performance in the face of failure.

It is not difficult to understand why differences were obtained between advantaged and disadvantaged children. Unlike many investigations of SES differences, in the present studies there was no overlap in SES between advantaged and disadvantaged groups but rather a sizeable gap between them in their parents' education, occupation, and income. In the typical groups study, the advantaged children also had higher IQs and MAs in comparison with the other children being studied. The advantaged children were very advantaged, while the disadvantaged children were likewise very disadvantaged. It is somewhat surprising, then, that more differences in behavior were not revealed.

In considering the differences in performance patterns between advantaged and disadvantaged children that have emerged in the investigation, it is clear the each can be viewed with both satisfaction and concern. The typical advantaged children excelled on many of the tasks presented them. What is of some concern, however, are those instances where typical advantaged children showed less fluency and flexibility on the Verbal Creativity tasks, and less self-confidence on the Balancing task than did typical disadvantaged children. These results, along with those on the dependency measures, suggest that typical advantaged children are achieving but anxious. While the advantaged children in the typical groups study were superior on standardized intellectual and achievement measures, they also seemed to pay a price in spontaneity and in a willingness to be seen as having made a mistake.

These children seemed unwilling to emit a "wrong" response on the creativity tasks, and they showed a constricted style, producing the absolutely lowest fluency and flexibility scores of any group studied. While they had considerable self-confidence on the Reading task, they were careful in approaching the Balancing task until they had determined that they could perform it adequately. On the Five-Objects task, they sat silently rather than tell the examiner that they could not find a suitable solution. The socialization pressures and expectations that produce this kind of approach to problem-solving must surely be intense. While such strategies may produce high achievement, these strategies may also produce a harmful overconformity.

In contrast, the typical disadvantaged children, although more spontaneous and flexible in their approach to problem-solving, appear to lack self-confidence on academic tasks. Evidence from the matched groups study showed that even when disadvantaged children are equal to advantaged children on IQ-test performance, they have less confidence in their academic skills. Given the equivalence of the disadvantaged children to the advantaged children on many measures and their excellence on some measures, this lowered self-confidence seems almost an anomaly. Since the disadvantaged children had lower school achievement (as will be discussed later), their lower self-confidence may reflect a realistic assessment of how they are likely to perform. What remains puzzling is why disadvantaged children should have lower school achievement than advantaged children of the same IQ and MA.

Finally, there may seem to be a paradox in comparing the results of the two studies. In the first study, IQ and MA appeared to be important determinants of SES differences, since when samples were matched on these variables SES differences virtually disappeared. In the second study, IQ and MA appeared to be unimportant, since SES differences continued to be found after these variables had been controlled by the covariance procedure. To some extent the explanation for these findings again lies in considering the nature of the samples compared. The advantaged children in the matched groups study seemed not to have developed the cautious, self-censoring style which characterized the academically more competent typical advantaged children. Among typical advantaged children this style was so marked, and it contrasted so strongly with the spontaneity and creativity of typical disadvantaged children, that the differences continued to be evident regardless of any statistical adjustments for IQ or MA differences.

Ethnic-Group and Sex Differences

Unlike the SES variable, very few significant differences were associated with ethnic-group membership. The overall findings of the present study thus lend further support to the view that in many studies ethnicity is confounded with SES, and if one examines ethnic differences independently of SES, few differences appear. In the matched groups study and in the typical groups study following covariance analyses, no performance differences between the ethnic groups were revealed. In the typical groups study prior to covariance analyses, only two findings emerged—one related to autonomy, the other to frustration threshold. Black children made fewer attempts on the Token-in-the-Box task and were more imitative on the Find-the-Surprise task. In light of the failure to find ethnic differences on any other measure, including the remaining frustration threshold and autonomy measures, an interpretation of these findings seems unwarranted. In general, SES was found to be a better predictor of performance than was ethnic-group membership.

Although no significant sex effects emerged in either of the multivariate analyses of variance (MANOVAs), a striking sex effect was found on one of the dependent measures, hand-holding requests on the Walk-the-Board task. In both the matched groups and typical groups studies, females made approximately twice as many requests for hand-holding as did males. Taken alone, the finding was highly significant in both studies ($p < .0001$). This finding is consistent with commonly held views on differences in the socialization of males and females (Maccoby & Jacklin, 1974). Given the broad range of behaviors investigated and the relatively large sample size, it is interesting that so few group differences were found to be associated with ethnicity or sex. Black and white children and males and females may behave more similarly than much previous literature would suggest.

CHILDREN'S INTERVIEW MEASURES

The most salient feature of the children's self-ratings was their predominantly positive quality. In both the matched and typical groups studies, the total self-concept scores of the children, regardless of SES, ethnicity, or sex, were found to be favorable. We recognize, however, that the question must remain open whether these generally high self-concept scores reflect real self-satisfaction or whether they reflect a socially desirable response (Crandall, 1966; Crowne & Marlowe, 1964). Research on how such a response bias might influence children's self-ratings would be of interest. Further, the skewed and relatively homogeneous characteristics of the self-concept scores obtained in this investigation would appear to lend support to the argument of Katz and Zigler (1967) that research on children's self-images should employ measures of both real and ideal self-image.

Of particular interest in the interview results is the lack of findings related to ethnicity. It has often been assumed that black children have lower self-concepts than white children. In a review of the literature on black and white differences in self-esteem, however, Rosenberg and Simmons (1971) concluded that existing studies as a whole showed no racial differences in self-esteem—a conclusion that they also drew from their own data. A fine-grained analysis of their data revealed, however, that factors such as the child's social context could modify this general conclusion. They found, for example, that black children who attended predominantly white schools had lower self-esteem than black children who attended predominantly black schools (a finding replicated in the present study on the experimental measure of self-confidence; see the section on racial composition of the schools). In general, then, the findings of the present investigation regarding ethnicity and self-esteem are consistent with previous evidence on this issue.

While no significant findings were obtained on the overall Self-Concept score in either study, in the typical groups study two of the individual items (possessions and strength) resulted in significant findings. Females, compared to males, were more likely to state that they liked their possessions. While it is not possible to be certain about the interpretation of a single finding such as this, it is possible that satisfaction with possessions is a socially desirable and adaptive response for females, who are seen by our culture as receiving good things not by their own actions but through the agency of others (Jacklin & Mischel, 1973). Socialization pressures would be different, then, for boys and girls on this measure. While there were no overall sex differences on whether the children perceived themselves as strong—a finding consistent with that reported by Goss (1968) for the same age group—there was a race by sex interaction on this item in the typical groups study. For females, no race differences were revealed. For males, a larger percentage of white than of black children reported they were "not strong." It appears that being strong may be more valued by black than by white male children. One can only conjecture as to the differences in socialization histories that result in black males putting such a particularly high value on physical strength. Surely the historical importance of physical strength for survival and employment in the black culture should not be overlooked.

Very few significant findings were obtained on the measure of the children's perceptions of how they were viewed by their teacher. In neither study was the total score on the Teacher Thinks interview found to be related to SES, ethnicity, or sex. Significant findings were obtained on two items in the typical groups study. Disadvantaged compared to advantaged children were more likely to state that their teachers believed they did not like their possessions. What exactly does it mean to a child to possess objects which are viewed as not valued by teachers? If a child has a sense that significant adults do not place much value on the child's possessions, the outcome could easily be self-disparagement. It is noteworthy, however, that few of the other esteem-related items in the Self-Concept scale showed class differences. It is possible that the possessions item does not measure self-esteem for disadvantaged children but instead reflects an early knowledge of their relative economic position in society. Certainly disadvantaged children are exposed to the economic frustrations of their parents and experience firsthand the fact that there is often not sufficient money in the family to spend on desired objects. That a child would assume that a teacher would not like his or her possessions is similar to a parent apologizing for the state of the furniture in the house when the teacher visits. The second significant finding was that females were more likely than were males to report that their teachers thought they liked their possessions. This sex difference appears to reflect a simple projection of the finding on the self-rating measure that females liked their possessions better than did males.

The children's self-ratings were compared with their perceptions of their teacher's ratings on the same items. Since both the Self-Concept responses and the Teacher Thinks responses were found to be positively skewed, it was not surprising to discover that the two sets of responses were related. For example, the children viewed themselves as being good and reported that their teacher viewed them as being good. The comparison of the Self-Concept and Teacher Thinks responses did disclose one interesting finding in the matched groups study. White children were more likely to report that teachers thought more highly of them than they thought of themselves, whereas black children reported no difference between self and teacher perceptions. This finding is surprising because it was obtained in a study in which white and black children were equated on IQ, a factor which was found to influence the teachers' ratings of the children. The finding may be related to the fact that the white advantaged children in the matched groups study had on the average lower IQs than the white advantaged children in the typical groups study. To the extent that these matched groups children compare themselves to their reference group (other white, and quite likely more capable children), they may underestimate their own abilities and consequently perceive their teachers as overrating them. Clearly more work is needed comparing the self-image of black and white children of varying IQ levels with these children's perceptions of their teachers' evaluations of them.

Relationship Between Interview Responses and Performance

Although the scores obtained on the children's Self-Concept and Teacher Thinks interviews were relatively homogeneous, several items from each of these rating scales were found to be related to the children's performance on the experimental tasks. The pattern of findings obtained in these analyses indicates that, in some instances, children appeared to be accurately aware of their behavior and were willing to report it. For example, the children's view that the teacher thought they "talked a lot" was positively related to the children's fluency score on the Verbal Creativity tasks and to the number of dependency statements they made on the Puzzle task. Children who were persistent and who asked for little help on the difficult Puzzle task reported that their teachers thought they were "strong." Interestingly, this self-report item was *negatively* related to the child's dependency on the Walk-the-Board task. Similarly, the child's belief that the teacher viewed him or her as "scared of things" was associated with lower self-confidence scores on the Reading task but higher self-confidence on the Balancing and Walk-the-Board tasks. Evidently children believe that to the teacher being "afraid" or "weak" means specifically "afraid of academic tasks." In the children's view, their teachers do not appear to place much value on physical skills and daring.

A number of self-rating items were related to measures of creativity. The general pattern of the relationship between the interview responses and performance on creativity measures was that the more creative children appeared to be more willing to say negative things about themselves (e.g., that they were not "good," that they did not "like their possessions"). Creative children also reported that their teachers viewed them somewhat negatively (e.g., as being "ugly" and "scared of things"). Such a pattern of negative self-image and a belief that one is not valued by teachers is consistent with the descriptions of creative elementary school children often provided in the literature (Torrance, 1965). The children's perceptions of their teachers' views also find some support in the actual teachers' ratings of the children (discussed in the next section), which indicate that teachers are likely to devalue some attributes of creative children.

TEACHER RATING SCALE

The findings on teachers' ratings of the children differed in the two studies. No significant effects were obtained in the matched groups study, whereas significant SES, ethnic-group, and sex effects were obtained in the typical groups study. However, in the typical groups study, SES effects—which invariably favored the advantaged child— were not significant when IQ was a covariate. This pattern indicates that teachers' ratings of children are determined heavily by the children's IQs. When IQ was controlled, either through a matched groups design or statistically through covariance, the teachers' ratings of children were found to be unrelated to SES. Teachers' ratings were also not found to be associated with ethnicity in the matched groups study. In the typical groups study, teachers' ratings were found to vary as a function of the child's ethnic-group membership, and this variation was not attenuated, but rather was enhanced, when the effects of differences in IQ between the groups were controlled through the covariance procedure.

Several interpretations can be offered for the finding in the typical groups study that black children were rated more positively by the teachers than were white children. There is evidence in prior studies that teachers rate more positively those children for whom they have lower expectations (Hillson & Myers, 1963; Rosenthal & Jacobson, 1968; Wilson, 1963). Wilson (1963), for example, conducted a study in which he compared children who attended schools that were divided into three social-class strata. He found, after taking into consideration differences in achievement and IQ, that teachers tended to underevaluate students in the upper-stratum schools (predominantly white professional families) and overevaluate students in the lower-stratum schools (predominently black working-class families). Wilson reasoned that more stringent demands were placed on students in the upper-stratum schools and that teachers had higher expectations for them. Another hypothesis is suggested by the fact that the present investigation was conducted during a period (1971–1972) of considerable racial strife. (The typical groups study was conducted during the most troubled of these times.) It is quite likely that the teachers, who knew they were participating in a research project, were strongly motivated to correct for any possible prejudices. Although the possibility exists that the teachers' ratings were an accurate reflection of the black children's actual classroom behavior, the findings from the present investigation do not support such a conclusion. Ethnic group differences were obtained on only two of the 26 experimental measures.

It is important to note that although the finding from the typical groups study suggests that teachers view black children more positively than white children, this finding was based upon rating scale data. No data were obtained on the relationship of the ratings to the grades actually given the children. Further, whether a teacher's stated evaluation is closely related to his or her behavioral interactions with children remains an open question. Some evidence suggests that it is not. Two observational studies (Coates, 1972; Rubovits & Maehr, 1973) in which teachers' expectancies were experimentally manipulated resulted in the finding that preferential treatment was given to white students. With reference to the present investigation, however, even if teachers did view black children more positively than white children, there is evidence that the white children did not perceive themselves as discriminated against. As previously reported in the section on the children's interviews, white children generally perceived their teachers' evaluations of them as more positive than their self-evaluations. One final comment can be made about the ethnic-group findings. A child's skin color, unfortunately, apparently continues to be a salient factor in the determination of teacher attitudes.

One significant sex effect was found on the teacher rating scale. Females were viewed by teachers as being more mature than males. This attitude on the part of teachers is consistent with the common view in our society that female children display a more accelerated maturity than do male children.

Teachers' Ratings and Children's Performance

A number of significant relationships were found between the teachers' ratings of children and the children's performance on the experimental measures. It was not surprising to find that the teachers' rating of classroom achievement was highly related to two of the three self-confidence measures on the Reading task. Ratings of classroom achievement were also positively related to two of the seven originality measures on the Creativity tasks and to the curiosity measure. Teachers also apparently value a child's neatness, a rating which was highly related to the two Reading task measures. Somewhat surprisingly, however, the neatness rating was negatively related to the fluency and flexibility measures of creativity. Classroom achievement was also negatively related to the fluency measure of creativity. Although consistent with the disheveled artist stereotype, these findings suggest that teachers do not value such behaviors in the classroom.

In view of the children's reports on the interview that their teachers viewed them as "scared of things" when in fact the children's performance indicated that they lacked self-confidence only on the Reading task (see p. 96), it is interesting that the teachers' ratings of children as "fearful of things" was related only to low self-confidence on the Reading task. Evidently the teachers viewed fearfulness specifically in terms of academic tasks, and the children accurately perceived their teachers' orientation on this matter.

Finally, although the teachers' rating of leadership was related to the overall Reading task measure, it was also positively related to one measure of dependency and negatively related to self-confidence on the Balancing task. This finding suggests that teachers may define leadership qualities quite differently than would commonly be expected (e.g., independence).

Lacking in the present investigation are indications of how much the teachers valued the attributes they were asked to rate. Teachers' ratings of children on a characteristic such as "fears things" offer no indication of whether teachers think that fearing things is a good or bad attribute. Uncovering such value systems could be important in further work on SES and ethnic group variation in children's performance. The value systems of teachers could then be compared to those of children from various SES and ethnic subgroups in order to determine the degree of congruency between them. One could then proceed to investigate whether the degree of congruency is related to the children's behavior.

FATHER'S PRESENCE OR ABSENCE

Few significant performance differences were found to be associated with the father-absence variable. Significant findings on the experimental measures were obtained only in the matched groups study, and these findings must be considered tentative since they were not replicated in the typical groups study.[2] The disadvantaged samples in the matched and typical groups studies were similar in IQ and MA. The fact that significant findings for the father-absence variable were obtained in only one study therefore does not appear to be due to sampling differences, as was the case in comparing the social-class groups. Rather, the matched groups study may simply have had more statistical power, as there were equal cell sizes and a slightly larger number of children being studied. Even with this greater power, the few significant findings associated with father-absence were significant at only the .05 level.

In the matched groups study, father-present children were found to be more creative than father-absent children on two of the nine creativity measures: the originality per response, and the highest originality measures on the Verbal Creativity tasks. They also chose an easier problem on their first attempt on the Balancing task, and they made fewer requests for feedback on the Five-Objects task. These findings are similar to those obtained for advantaged children in the typical groups study. The father-present children's behavior thus can be seen to resemble the cautious problem-solving style characteristic of the typical groups advantaged children (who had fathers present). Inasmuch as this style of problem-solving is advantageous to performance in academic settings, these findings can be interpreted as supportive of Bronfenbrenner's (1975) argument that two-parent homes provide a more optimal environment for development than a single-parent home.

On the interviews, again few significant findings were obtained. Children from the typical groups study who came from father-absent homes reported not liking other children, and they believed that their teachers did not think they were smart. While these findings may be indications of low self-esteem, they represent only two out of 28 possible findings in the interview data. The teachers' ratings provide some confirmation that the teachers do in fact believe that certain groups of father-absent children are less capable than their father-present counterparts. The picture is complicated by the fact that the teachers may be using somewhat different standards depending upon the child's

---

[2]Generalization of the findings is also limited by the fact that the samples were selected employing a simple dichotomy of father presence or absence. Consideration of such factors as duration of absence, reason for absence, and temporary or continuing absence (Herzog & Sudia, 1973; Lamb, 1976) would have been preferable but was not possible within the scope of the present investigation.

race and sex: Teachers rated father-absent white females as less curious than their father-present counterparts, and rated father-absent black males as lower in reading ability than father-present black males. While the differences between the sexes in school achievement did not attain significance, the direction of the difference was consistent with these differences in teacher ratings: That is, white females showed lower school achievement than did white males, and black males showed lower achievement than did black females. Perhaps teachers look to father-absence as an explanation for these children's poorer academic performance.

The overall paucity of differences obtained in the comparison of disadvantaged children from father-present homes with disadvantaged children from father-absent homes lends some support to the argument, raised in one review of the literature (Herzog & Sudia, 1973), that a father's presence or absence may have less impact on the child's development than has often been believed. On the other hand, there were no findings in the present investigation to suggest that a father's absence is a positive experience for the growing child.

SCHOOL RACIAL COMPOSITION

The analyses of school racial composition were based upon relatively small samples of black, disadvantaged children. Although no significant findings were obtained in the typical groups study, some findings associated with racial composition of the schools were obtained in the matched groups study. The difference in the results of the two studies may have been due to the difference in IQs of the samples. The disadvantaged black children in the matched groups study had a mean IQ over half a standard deviation higher than the mean IQ of the comparable children in the typical groups study.

In the matched groups study, disadvantaged black children who attended predominantly black schools obtained higher scores than disadvantaged black children who attended predominantly white schools on four of the seven self-confidence measures, and they made more requests for feedback on the Five-Objects tasks. This last finding is somewhat difficult to interpret, because it might reflect either positive or negative aspects of the child's functioning. Children who requested feedback on the Five-Objects tasks could be considered to lack confidence in their ability to do the task. However, a more positive feature of the behavior is suggested by the fact that the Five-Objects task requires the child to ask for assistance in the face of failure. Such behavior may indicate that the child senses his or her requests for help or counsel will be tolerated and responded to with approbation. The hypothesis can thus be generated that black children in predominantly black schools feel more accepted by the adults and peers in their school environment than do black children who attend predominantly white schools. The self-confidence findings described above are consistent with this interpretation.

The finding of greater self-confidence among disadvantaged black children in predominantly black schools in comparison with those in predominantly white schools is consistent with results from several other studies (see reviews by Rosenberg & Simmons, 1971; St. John, 1975). The literature in this area, however, is limited and somewhat contradictory. For example, although St. John and Smith (1969) found that black children in segregated schools had higher educational aspirations than black children in integrated schools, Veroff and Peele (1969) found that after a year of desegregation black males bused to predominantly white schools increased in achievement motivation and became more moderate in risk-taking (a finding not obtained for females). Apart from the dissimilarities in measurement and method-ology, these two studies make clear the need for longitudinal data before the short- and long-term effects of desegregation can be disentangled. These few studies, as well as the findings from the present investigation, suggest that the further exploration of personality and motivational variables in the assessment of the effects of the racial composition of schools is a promising avenue of research. As Zigler (1973) has repeatedly argued, motivational factors have been under-explored in studies of disadvantaged children, while an inordinate amount of effort has been expended in assessing formal intelligence and achievement variables.

Two significant findings were obtained on the nonperformance measures—again in the matched groups study. Both of these findings, one obtained from the children's interviews and the other from the teachers' ratings, provide further support for the hypothesis that black children in predominantly black schools feel accepted by persons in their environment. On the interview data, black children who attended predominently black schools were more likely than were black children who attended predominantly white schools to report that their teachers thought more highly of them than they thought of themselves. Further, black children in predominantly black schools were in fact rated higher on classroom achievement by their teachers than were black children in predominantly white schools. This difference in ratings is somewhat surprising since the two groups did not differ on their actual level of reading and arithmetic achievement (see next section for a discussion of these findings) or in chronological age, MA, or IQ. However, the children in the predominantly white schools were likely to be in classrooms with high-achieving advantaged children, whereas the children in predominantly black schools were probably not. The simple difference in reference group could account for the findings. In addition, teachers in predominantly white schools may expect more of their students.

DEMOGRAPHIC AND STANDARDIZED TEST MEASURES

Sample Comparisons

As noted previously, the samples in the matched groups study were presumed to be atypical because of the constraints introduced by IQ and MA matching and the restriction of subjects to children who had not repeated a grade in school. It was not surprising, therefore, that a comparison of the samples from the matched and typical groups studies indicated that they differed on the IQ, MA, and school retention variables. Surprisingly, however, these were the only background variables on which the matched and typical studies samples differed. The advantaged children in the matched groups study had significantly lower IQs than did the typical groups advantaged children, and the white children in the matched groups study had significantly lower IQs than did the typical groups white children. (Differences in MA were in the same direction, but they did not attain statistical significance.) Although the disadvantaged children and the black children in the matched groups study tended to have higher IQs and MAs than did their typical sample counterparts, the differences were not significant. Father-present samples in the two studies also did not differ significantly on any background variable, including IQ and MA. The same was true of the father-absent samples.

SES, Ethnic-Group, and Sex Comparisons Within Each Study

The data on busing children to school and on the degree of ethnic mixture in the schools suggest that the experiences of the advantaged black children were somewhat unusual. In both studies, advantaged black children were the only groups of children who were likely to attend schools in which they were a distinct minority; they were also more likely than other groups of children to be bused to school. Such experiences may well lead to a feeling of being special or different, with the possibility of both positive and negative connotations of such a difference. The findings also suggest that the advantaged black families may be especially striving and upwardly mobile. In both studies, advantaged black children had fewer siblings than did other groups of children (significantly so in the typical groups study); such smaller family size is a sociological variable often associated with upward mobility.

In the typical groups study, significant SES and ethnic-group IQ differences were obtained. Advantaged children scored approximately 12 points higher than disadvantaged children, and white children scored approximately 12 points higher than black children. No ethnic-group findings were obtained on the school achievement data. Comparison of groups on these data, however, yielded the troublesome and consistent finding that, even with differences in MA and IQ controlled (by matching or by covariance), disadvantaged children had significantly poorer reading achievement scores than did advantaged children. In both studies, disadvantaged children were seven months behind advantaged children in reading level by the middle of their third-grade years. Data for arithmetic achievement were available for fewer children than were reading scores, and the results should therefore be considered more tentative. Again, however, disadvantaged children were clearly behind advantaged children in their achievement, with disadvantaged black children particularly so. The data on school retention also indicated poorer achievement by disadvantaged than by advantaged children.

There are a number of reasons to interpret the school achievement data with caution. Nevertheless, the consistency of the findings across both studies and a variety of tests is impressive. It unfortunately indicates that disadvantaged children early in their school experience show a markedly lower level of achievement than would be predicted on the basis of their aptitude scores. Why these findings exist, of course, is open to question and cannot be answered by the present investigation. The present investigation does, however, suggest that disadvantaged children have some behavioral styles which can be misunderstood by teachers. If such is the case, the lack of appropriate teaching strategies for disadvantaged children could contribute to their failure to achieve. Clearly more research is needed.

Father's Presence or Absence;
Racial Composition of the Schools

A comparison of father-present with father-absent children on demographic and standardized-test-performance measures yielded only one significant finding: in the matched groups sample, black children from father-absent homes had more siblings than did white children from father-absent homes. As was true for comparisons of father-present and father-absent children on the experimental measures, there was little indication of any effects of this variable on the nonexperimentally administered measures.

In examining the data on school racial composition in the typical groups study, black children who attended predominantly white schools were found to be older than black children who attended predominantly black schools. This appeared to be partially a random sampling error, and partially the result of having tested more children in predominantly white schools later in the year rather than earlier. The groups did not differ in IQ or on other background measures. There were differences in achievement, however: Even with effects of MA statistically controlled, typical disadvantaged black children who attended predominantly white schools had higher achievement scores than did comparable children who attended predominantly black schools. (Since the achievement scores were adjusted for the time when the child was seen in the present study, differences in time of testing did not account for the achievement differences obtained.) Although this finding is consistent with those reported in the literature on school integration (for a review, see Mosteller & Moynihan, 1972; St. John, 1975), in the present investigation, the selection factors for students who attended predominantly white schools was unknown. Therefore, whether the children were chosen to attend these schools on the basis of their achievement or whether their higher achievement was the result of being in predominantly white schools cannot be determined. In the matched groups study, there were no differences on IQ, MA, achievement, or any other variable between the children who attended predominantly black and those who attended predominantly white schools.

The difference between the results of the matched and typical groups studies deserves comment. As noted earlier, the matched groups disadvantaged black children, regardless of the type of school they attended, had higher IQs and MAs than did the typical groups disadvantaged black children. In the matched groups study, no evidence was found that the racial composition of the school was associated with academic achievement, but there was evidence of a negative association with the children's self-confidence. In contrast, for children in the typical groups study, attending a predominantly white school was associated with higher academic achievement but had no other evident effects. These results suggest that the consequences of school integration may be very complex. It must be emphasized that our data are merely suggestive for further research, and cannot be said to have evaluated the effects of school integration. To do so, future studies must control for the degree of racial mixing in the school, the length of time a school has been integrated, and the circumstances of the integration (i.e., as reflecting the neighborhood or achieved through busing), as well as standard controls on such variables as social class and teacher ratios.

SUMMARY AND CONCLUSIONS

The results of the present investigation have both methodological and substantive implications. Methodologically, the present studies indicate that in the investigation of SES and ethnic-group differences, the best strategy is to employ random samples and to control statistically for MA and IQ by the use of covariance procedures. The major substantive findings were:

1. Differences associated with social-class membership were far more extensive than differences associated with ethnic-group membership.
2. Differences which were obtained, as predicted, were not unidirectional, and patterns of performance emerged for each SES group.
3. Neither SES nor ethnic-group differences were obtained on children's overall self-ratings.
4. Teachers' ratings of children were influenced both by the children's IQ and ethnic-group membership.
5. Few differences of any kind—in behavior, interview reports, or ratings—were found between disadvantaged children from father-absent and father-present homes.
6. The racial composition of the schools attended by disadvantaged black children seemed to have mixed effects—attending integrated schools may have affected school achievement (positively) for some children and self-confidence (negatively) for others.

Perhaps the clearest finding of the present investigation is that no one group of children performed uniformly better than any other group when their performance was examined across a wide variety of problem-solving situations. Furthermore, when group differences did emerge, they were more likely to reflect stylistic patterns rather than capacity differences. The present results add to the argument that a better understanding of children in our society who are not middle-class white children can be gained only if we attempt to devise measures and define situations that allow their competencies to emerge (Baratz & Baratz, 1970; Cole & Bruner, 1971; Hertzig et al., 1968; Labov, 1970). Even though the present investigation was not conducted within a naturalistic setting, the examination of a wide array of behaviors, the use of a large number of measures, and the emphasis on nonconventional rather than traditional academic problem-solving tasks revealed important information about the variations in problem-solving strategies of children from different SES backgrounds. Nevertheless, the testing was conducted in school settings; thus the present findings may provide only a conservative picture of the stylistic differences to be found among such groups of children.

Important evidence was found that on a number of measures disadvantaged and advantaged children showed great similarity, even though the differences in the socioeconomic circumstances in which they were being raised were considerable. Furthermore, disadvantaged children were found to be particularly able on tasks requiring creative thinking. The point to be made is not, of course, that there is an advantage to children in being raised under deprived economic circumstances. Rather, it is that the results of this investigation suggest that children can respond to economic privation by developing a complex pattern of resiliencies and strengths as well as weaknesses in comparison with children from more advantaged backgrounds.

The present findings were derived from groups of children who apparently had had little exposure to children from other social-class and racial backgrounds. Few of the children, with the exception of the advantaged black children, were bused to school, and most of the neighborhoods in which the children resided were homogeneous both ethnically and socioeconomically. The SES differences obtained in the present investigation should therefore be viewed against the background of school and social segregation which existed in 1971 and 1972. Changes in the diversity of school populations over the past few years represent a change in social conditions such that the results of the present investigation, if conducted today, might be somewhat different.

Given the aims of the present investigation, however, it was advantageous that relatively isolated groups of children could be studied. The present research can also be considered to be a preliminary step to a study of the effects of exposure to social diversity upon children's behaviors and attitudes.

Inasmuch as the present investigation is discrepant in approach (difference vs. deficit) with the larger body of research on SES and ethnic-group differences and because new conceptualizations of the influence of social class on problem-solving have emerged, there are implications for future research. If we are to better understand the similarities and variations in children's adaptive functioning, it will be necessary to study a wider range of behaviors and to extend research investigations to those areas of a child's experiences which are outside the academic environment. The search for factors which contribute to the academic failure of certain groups of children, even if undertaken for the worthwhile purpose of ameliorating such problems, has produced little more than the stereotype of the "deficient" child. What is "wrong" with a child or what is "missing" from a child's environment rarely provides information about how a child learns and adapts. To help children learn it is necessary to understand how and under what circumstances they do so. Variations in how children learn obviously do exist. Once uncovered, these variations can be used as the structure around which teaching strategies are designed—not only for the purpose of enabling all children to meet necessary educational standards, but, more importantly, to foster unique achievement.

Appendixes

Self-Concept Interview

Directions. "Now, as I told you earlier, the game company I work for wants to make games that boys and girls like, and we'd like to know more about kids your age so we can make better games. That's why we ask them questions about themselves. Now I'd like to ask *you* some questions about yourself, about (child's name), OK?"

Items.
1. "Is (child's name) scared of people or is (he or she) not scared of people?"
2. "Is (child's name) sick or is (he or she) well?"
3. "Does (child's name) like his or her face, or doesn't (he or she) like (his or her) face?"
4. "Does (child's name) talk a lot or doesn't (he or she) talk a lot?"
5. "Is (child's name) smart or is (he or she) dumb?"
6. "Is (child's name) scared of things or isn't (he or she) scared of things?"
7. "Is (child's name) good or is (he or she) bad?"

8. "Does (child's name) like other kids or doesn't (he or she) like other kids?"
9. "Does (child's name) like the things (he or she) has or doesn't (he or she) like (his or her) things?"
10. "Is (child's name) ugly or is (he or she) good-looking?"
11. "Is (child's name) strong or is (he or she) weak?"
12. "Is (child's name) happy or is (he or she) sad?"
13. "Is (child's name) clean or is (he or she) dirty?"
14. "Does (child's name) like (his or her) clothes or doesn't (he or she) like (his or her) clothes?"

Teacher Thinks Interview

Directions. "Now I'd like to ask you some more questions. This time I'd like to ask you a few questions about your teacher. What's her name?"

Items.
1. "Now, do you suppose that (teacher's name) thinks that (child's name) is scared of people or that (he or she) isn't scared of people?"
2. "Do you suppose that (teacher's name) thinks that (child's name) is sick or that (he or she) is well?"

[The remaining 12 items were equivalent (a) in form to the questions just presented, and (b) in content to those in the Self-Concept Interview.]

Mean Values and Standard Deviations for Each Group on Each Measure: Matched Groups Study

Measure	Advantaged								Disadvantaged							
	Black Females (N = 12)		Black Males (N = 12)		White Females (N = 12)		White Males (N = 12)		Black Females (N = 12)		Black Males (N = 12)		White Females (N = 12)		White Males (N = 12)	
	$\bar{X}$	SD	$\bar{X}$	SD	$\bar{X}$	SD	$\bar{X}$	SD	$\bar{X}$	SD	$\bar{X}$	SD	$\bar{X}$	SD	$\bar{X}$	SD
Verbal Creativity:																
Originality per response	2.52	.66	3.22	.46	3.11	.81	3.22	.59	2.88	.74	3.09	.72	2.86	.52	3.25	.77
Highest originality	3.67	1.20	4.54	.71	4.40	.92	4.58	.61	4.29	.87	4.40	.76	4.48	.93	4.17	.84
Fluency	8.50	3.45	9.54	3.60	7.00	2.51	7.88	3.39	10.67	4.69	8.71	2.02	9.54	3.15	6.96	3.31
Flexibility	4.08	2.07	4.25	1.54	4.08	1.15	4.04	1.15	4.67	1.84	4.79	1.31	5.00	1.47	3.62	1.84
Dog and Bone:																
Quality per path	.88	.46	1.06	.29	1.12	.43	1.10	.42	.96	.41	1.32	.61	1.15	.52	1.31	.59
Highest quality	2.00	.71	2.42	.49	2.50	.64	2.33	.47	2.17	.80	2.33	.62	2.33	.62	2.25	.72
Token-in-the-Box:																
Quality per attempt	3.56	.80	4.06	.98	3.87	.86	3.56	.96	3.34	.82	4.02	1.18	3.58	1.48	3.14	1.06
Highest quality	6.00	.91	6.42	1.04	6.33	.85	6.25	.92	5.33	1.65	5.83	1.46	5.33	1.97	4.92	1.98
Five-Objects:																
Highest number	4.58	.49	4.67	.62	4.08	1.38	4.08	.86	4.75	.60	4.42	.64	4.17	1.34	4.42	.76
Reading:																
First attempt	1.83	.69	1.75	.92	2.00	.58	1.75	.60	1.25	.60	1.67	.85	1.33	.47	1.25	.43
Mean attempt	1.85	.36	1.76	.47	1.96	.31	1.75	.31	1.53	.44	1.68	.47	1.64	.34	1.79	.28
Risk	11.50	2.84	11.17	2.70	11.17	2.48	11.92	2.25	10.83	3.31	11.58	3.35	12.00	1.92	11.42	3.40
Balancing:																
First attempt	1.67	.74	2.08	.76	2.08	.64	2.00	.82	1.67	.85	1.50	.64	1.75	.83	1.67	.74
Mean attempt	1.64	.24	1.96	.33	1.87	.26	1.76	.39	1.74	.27	1.78	.18	1.86	.24	1.82	.28
Risk	11.50	2.29	15.00	2.38	14.50	2.22	12.42	2.36	14.08	3.45	14.00	2.00	14.17	2.23	15.17	3.80
Token-in-the-Box:																
Percent expecting success	91.67	—	100.00	—	75.00	—	83.33	—	50.00	—	83.33	—	66.67	—	75.00	—

(continued)

111

APPENDIX B: (continued)

Measure	Advantaged								Disadvantaged							
	Black Females (N = 12)		Black Males (N = 12)		White Females (N = 12)		White Males (N = 12)		Black Females (N = 12)		Black Males (N = 12)		White Females (N = 12)		White Males (N = 12)	
	$\bar{X}$	SD	$\bar{X}$	SD	$\bar{X}$	SD	$\bar{X}$	SD	$\bar{X}$	SD	$\bar{X}$	SD	$\bar{X}$	SD	$\bar{X}$	SD
Find-the-Surprise:																
Percent with autonomous first choice	58.33	—	41.67	—	58.33	—	41.67	—	50.00	—	58.33	—	50.00	—	50.00	—
Total autonomous responses	2.50	1.56	2.08	1.26	2.25	1.23	2.00	1.35	2.33	1.37	2.67	1.25	2.50	1.44	1.83	1.28
Opening Doors:																
Number blank	7.67	4.70	9.42	4.42	10.67	3.17	9.83	2.76	6.83	4.79	7.50	5.74	8.42	5.12	9.67	2.69
Dog and Bone:																
Time to frustration	155.17	63.76	119.75	45.20	161.50	69.82	135.58	62.05	148.92	74.86	137.92	59.10	171.83	147.98	154.25	48.88
Token-in-the-Box:																
Number of attempts	21.75	7.89	19.75	7.69	20.25	6.35	19.33	5.53	21.25	9.66	18.17	7.92	16.83	6.72	14.67	7.72
Puzzle:																
Total time	180.00	0.00	173.50	21.56	180.00	0.00	177.33	8.84	176.58	9.66	170.50	22.62	180.00	0.00	176.75	10.78
Walk-the-Board:																
Handholding requests	15.33	6.02	6.00	7.25	12.33	6.37	7.88	8.62	13.83	7.00	5.92	8.21	12.08	7.35	9.33	8.54
Puzzle:																
Dependency statements per minute	.24	.30	.24	.30	.18	.24	.24	.36	.54	.54	.54	.54	.18	.24	.30	.36
Five-Objects:																
Requests for feedback	5.00	4.02	6.50	5.53	5.25	5.46	5.83	6.35	3.92	3.33	3.92	2.43	5.42	3.38	3.17	1.68
Percent needing prompting	8.33	—	16.67	—	16.67	—	8.33	—	16.67	—	8.33	—	16.67	—	16.67	—
Self-Concept:																
Total score	13.25	1.36	13.08	.95	14.00	0.00	13.42	1.11	13.67	1.49	13.33	1.25	13.75	1.42	14.00	0.00
Teacher Thinks:																
Total score	12.83	1.14	13.00	.82	13.33	1.03	13.00	.91	13.58	1.50	13.08	.86	12.75	.60	13.58	2.02
Teacher Ratings:																
Total score	54.00	5.94	51.46	5.76	53.83	5.03	47.50	5.65	45.75	7.24	50.58	5.92	51.00	10.15	48.42	8.28

Mean Values and Standard Deviations for Each Group on Each Measure: Typical Groups Study

	Advantaged								Disadvantaged							
	Black Females (N = 20)		Black Males (N = 20)		White Females (N = 20)		White Males (N = 20)		Black Females (N = 20)		Black Males (N = 20)		White Females (N = 20)		White Males (N = 20)	
Measure	X̄	SD	X̄	SD	X̄	SD	X̄	SD	X̄	SD	X̄	SD	X̄	SD	X̄	SD
Verbal Creativity:																
Originality per response	3.23	.70	3.09	.79	2.93	.76	3.21	.81	2.24	.49	2.91	.78	2.73	.63	2.87	.56
Highest originality	4.25	.91	4.21	.94	3.95	1.02	4.28	1.22	3.48	.93	4.27	1.16	3.84	.88	3.85	.81
Fluency	7.08	3.68	9.85	4.41	7.72	4.50	7.95	3.36	11.33	4.29	8.95	4.04	9.98	4.06	10.85	4.17
Flexibility	3.22	1.05	4.22	1.88	3.40	1.52	3.45	1.38	4.38	1.75	4.32	1.81	4.42	2.01	4.35	1.81
Dog and Bone:																
Quality per path	1.24	.46	1.46	.46	1.27	.52	1.33	.52	1.08	.45	1.24	.42	.90	.55	1.13	.50
Highest quality	2.30	.64	2.70	.46	2.50	.59	2.40	.74	2.25	.43	2.55	.50	2.00	.71	2.35	.65
Token-in-the-Box:																
Quality per attempt	3.95	1.13	3.74	1.37	3.38	.94	3.78	1.21	3.68	1.12	3.87	.84	3.64	1.04	3.82	1.35
Highest quality	6.20	1.44	5.65	1.59	5.35	1.71	6.00	1.38	5.90	1.38	5.90	.94	5.80	1.25	6.00	1.22
Five-Objects:																
Highest number	4.45	.86	4.50	.74	4.60	.66	4.35	.91	4.40	.74	4.45	.59	4.55	.74	4.25	.77
Reading:																
First attempt	1.65	.73	1.80	.81	1.85	.79	1.85	.73	1.30	.64	1.55	.74	1.05	.22	1.30	.46
Mean attempt	1.98	.48	1.81	.49	2.02	.46	2.00	.47	1.66	.30	1.58	.34	1.64	.38	1.73	.28
Risk	13.20	2.42	11.80	2.56	11.35	2.17	12.55	2.31	13.20	2.42	12.90	3.92	12.90	3.43	13.35	1.98
Balancing:																
First attempt	1.60	.66	1.80	.81	1.75	.70	1.70	.71	2.25	.77	1.70	.78	1.80	.81	2.25	.83
Mean attempt	1.83	.29	1.85	.26	1.87	.34	1.79	.34	1.90	.24	1.82	.23	1.79	.29	1.98	.22
Risk	13.95	2.92	13.55	3.25	13.55	2.69	13.60	2.35	12.60	2.50	14.15	2.39	13.55	3.09	14.05	2.50
Token-in-the-Box:																
Percent expecting success	85.00	—	65.00	—	85.00	—	90.00	—	80.00	—	95.00	—	85.00	—	100.00	—

(continued)

APPENDIX C: (continued)

Measure	Advantaged								Disadvantaged							
	Black Females (N = 20)		Black Males (N = 20)		White Females (N = 20)		White Males (N = 20)		Black Females (N = 20)		Black Males (N = 20)		White Females (N = 20)		White Males (N = 20)	
	X̄	SD	X̄	SD	X̄	SD	X̄	SD	X̄	SD	X̄	SD	X̄	SD	X̄	SD
Find-the-Surprise:																
Percent with autonomous first choice	60.00	—	65.00	—	65.00	—	75.00	—	50.00	—	60.00	—	80.00	—	75.00	—
Total autonomous responses	2.70	1.27	2.30	1.27	2.55	1.28	2.80	1.08	2.20	1.25	2.30	1.31	3.20	1.08	2.60	1.24
Opening Doors: Number blank	9.90	3.18	7.85	4.55	10.50	2.20	10.30	2.67	6.55	3.85	8.05	4.18	7.85	5.27	8.55	4.39
Dog and Bone: Time to frustration	151.80	64.46	155.85	60.04	178.60	118.10	132.15	45.25	144.90	53.53	158.15	67.79	119.40	53.18	141.25	54.68
Token-in-the-Box: Number of attempts	16.00	6.13	18.55	8.67	19.90	7.31	17.35	8.07	17.80	6.92	18.10	7.56	25.25	8.98	19.25	6.74
Puzzle: Total time	173.75	20.41	173.30	20.89	175.20	14.40	176.60	10.22	173.25	15.59	175.70	14.37	180.00	0.00	178.60	5.66
Walk-the-Board: Handholding requests	11.20	7.63	12.05	7.65	10.70	7.95	6.40	7.98	13.35	6.46	5.80	7.99	14.55	5.95	8.25	7.74
Puzzle: Dependency statements per minute	.36	.60	.24	.36	.30	.60	.24	.30	.60	.48	.48	.60	.54	.48	.42	.54
Five-Objects: Requests for feedback	5.00	3.90	5.90	2.91	2.85	2.48	3.20	2.16	5.95	4.76	4.50	2.96	7.25	7.91	5.85	3.80
Percent needing prompting	0.00	—	0.00	—	30.00	—	30.00	—	5.00	—	10.00	—	0.00	—	5.00	—
Self-Concept: Total score	13.85	1.24	13.65	1.96	13.25	1.73	13.55	1.46	13.70	1.27	13.45	1.02	13.35	1.46	13.65	2.22
Teacher Thinks: Total score	13.20	1.54	13.05	.74	13.00	1.00	13.05	1.02	13.30	1.14	13.20	1.21	13.05	1.28	13.60	2.01
Teacher Ratings: Total score	55.20	9.61	51.50	8.13	51.35	8.37	52.65	11.36	49.30	6.29	51.95	9.11	46.80	9.38	46.05	5.02

APPENDIX D:
RESULTS OF FACTOR ANALYSIS
OF TEACHERS' RATINGS

A principal components factor analysis of the teachers' ratings for the 304 children yielded four factors which accounted for 75.4% of the total variance. Each individual factor accounted for at least 5% of the variance. The factors were rotated employing an orthogonal varimax criterion. The loadings of each rating on each rotated factor are presented in Table D.1.

As can be seen in Table D.1, each of the four factors was reasonably simple to interpret. Factor 1, which accounted for nearly half of the variance, reflected the teachers' ratings of classroom achievement, with high-achieving children also rated as more mature and more persistent. Factors 2 and 4 can be considered self-confidence and neatness factors, respectively (high scores on fearfulness ratings denoted a lack of fearfulness). The remaining factor, Factor 3, seemed to indicate a general halo effect of all remaining positive qualities. The teachers therefore appeared to make only four rather than 12 independent ratings of children: achievement, self-confidence, an overall social style, and neatness.

TABLE D.1
Rotated Factor Loadings for Each Teacher Rating Variable
(N = 304)

Teacher Rating	Factor			
	1	2	3	4
Classroom achievement	.90	—[a]	—	—
Reading ability	.87	—	—	—
Creativity	—	—	.72	—
Maturity	.51	—	.56	—
Independence	—	—	.62	—
Curiosity	—	—	.75	—
Leadership	—	—	.80	—
Peer popularity	—	—	.74	—
Persistence	.61	—	—	—
Neatness	—	—	—	.94
Fearful of people	—	.93	—	—
Fearful of things	—	.94	—	—
[Percent of variance accounted for]	[45.4]	[14.4]	[8.5]	[7.0]

[a]Loadings with absolute values less than .50 are omitted for ease of interpretation.

APPENDIX E:
Mean Values and Standard Deviations for Each Measure for Father-Present and Father-Absent Disadvantaged Children: Matched Groups Study

Measure	Black Females				Black Males				White Females				White Males			
	Father-Present (N = 12)		Father-Absent (N = 12)		Father-Present (N = 12)		Father-Absent (N = 12)		Father-Present (N = 12)		Father-Absent (N = 12)		Father-Present (N = 12)		Father-Absent (N = 12)	
	$\bar{X}$	SD	$\bar{X}$	SD	$\bar{X}$	SD	$\bar{X}$	SD	$\bar{X}$	SD	$\bar{X}$	SD	$\bar{X}$	SD	$\bar{X}$	SD
Verbal Creativity:																
Originality per response	2.38	.74	2.39	.62	3.09	.72	2.84	.69	2.86	.52	2.47	.70	3.25	.77	2.98	.74
Highest originality	4.29	.87	3.46	1.03	4.40	.76	4.12	.65	4.48	.93	3.67	1.05	4.17	.84	4.27	.77
Fluency	10.67	4.69	11.79	6.19	8.71	2.02	9.25	2.71	9.54	3.15	10.38	5.34	6.96	3.31	10.46	4.04
Flexibility	4.67	1.84	3.17	1.08	4.79	1.31	3.96	.92	5.00	1.47	4.22	1.23	3.62	1.84	4.33	1.98
Dog and Bone:																
Quality per path	.96	.41	1.23	.54	1.32	.61	.72	.20	1.15	.52	1.13	.44	1.31	.59	1.07	.37
Highest quality	2.17	.80	2.50	.50	2.33	.62	1.75	.60	2.33	.62	2.42	.76	2.25	.72	2.17	.55
Token-in-the-Box:																
Quality per attempt	3.34	.82	3.37	1.29	4.02	1.18	3.93	.72	3.58	1.48	3.03	.88	3.14	1.06	3.48	.93
Highest quality	5.33	1.65	5.17	1.99	5.83	1.46	6.25	.92	5.33	1.97	5.42	1.38	4.92	1.98	5.83	1.46
Five-Objects:																
Highest number	4.75	.60	4.33	1.03	4.42	.64	4.50	.50	4.17	1.34	4.08	.95	4.42	.76	4.58	.86
Reading:																
First attempt	1.25	.60	1.25	.60	1.67	.85	1.17	.55	1.33	.47	1.58	.76	1.25	.43	2.00	.82
Mean attempt	1.53	.44	1.72	.32	1.68	.47	1.47	.34	1.64	.34	2.06	.37	1.79	.28	1.83	.41
Risk	10.83	3.31	13.33	2.10	11.58	3.35	11.00	3.46	12.00	1.92	13.58	1.98	11.42	3.40	11.67	1.84
Balancing:																
First attempt	1.67	.85	1.75	.72	1.50	.64	1.83	.80	1.75	.83	2.17	.69	1.67	.74	2.33	.74
Mean attempt	1.74	.27	1.79	.28	1.78	.18	1.71	.26	1.86	.24	1.85	.28	1.82	.28	1.96	.29
Risk	14.08	3.45	13.00	2.71	14.00	2.00	12.53	3.04	14.17	2.23	14.00	3.02	15.17	3.80	14.50	2.69
Token-in-the-Box:																
Percent expecting success	50.00	—	66.67	—	83.33	—	75.00	—	66.67	—	91.67	—	75.00	—	91.67	—

(continued)

Measure	Black Females				Black Males				White Females				White Males			
	Father-Present (N = 12)		Father-Absent (N = 12)		Father-Present (N = 12)		Father-Absent (N = 12)		Father-Present (N = 12)		Father-Absent (N = 12)		Father-Present (N = 12)		Father-Absent (N = 12)	
	$\bar{X}$	SD	$\bar{X}$	SD	$\bar{X}$	SD	$\bar{X}$	SD	$\bar{X}$	SD	$\bar{X}$	SD	$\bar{X}$	SD	$\bar{X}$	SD
Find-the-Surprise: Percent with autonomous first choice	50.00	—	58.33	—	58.33	—	41.67	—	50.00	—	58.33	—	50.00	—	66.67	—
Total autonomous responses	2.33	1.37	2.25	1.36	2.67	1.25	2.17	1.52	2.50	1.44	2.75	1.09	1.83	1.28	2.92	1.04
Opening Doors: Number blank	6.83	4.79	6.50	5.91	7.50	5.74	7.00	4.69	8.42	5.12	9.08	2.33	9.67	2.69	5.58	5.80
Dog and Bone: Time to frustration	148.92	74.86	127.08	41.64	137.92	59.10	124.67	40.97	171.83	147.98	145.67	51.76	154.25	48.88	112.17	65.84
Token-in-the-Box: Number of attempts	21.25	9.66	19.58	9.59	18.17	7.92	15.50	7.54	16.83	6.72	21.75	8.33	14.67	7.72	19.00	7.45
Puzzle: Total time	176.58	9.66	169.08	30.19	170.50	22.62	175.00	16.58	180.00	0.00	174.75	17.41	176.75	10.78	180.00	0.00
Walk-the-Board: Handholding requests	13.83	7.00	12.33	7.17	5.92	8.21	5.58	7.61	12.08	7.35	10.50	7.96	9.33	8.54	5.17	7.01
Puzzle: Dependency statements per minute	.54	.54	.42	1.02	.54	.54	.36	.36	.18	.24	.42	.36	.30	.36	.24	.30
Five-Objects: Requests for feedback	3.92	3.33	7.83	6.30	3.92	2.43	6.75	5.89	5.42	3.38	5.92	4.63	3.17	1.68	3.92	1.66
Percent needing prompting	16.67	—	0.00	—	8.33	—	0.00	—	16.67	—	16.67	—	16.67	—	0.00	—
Self-Concept: Total score	13.67	1.49	13.42	.76	13.33	1.25	13.33	1.11	13.75	1.42	14.00	0.00	14.00	0.00	14.00	0.00
Teacher Thinks: Total score	13.58	1.50	12.50	.50	13.08	.86	13.25	1.30	12.75	.60	13.75	1.59	13.58	2.02	13.50	1.89
Teacher Ratings: Total score	45.75	7.24	54.92	9.22	50.58	5.92	47.75	8.82	51.00	10.15	47.00	6.92	48.42	8.28	43.33	7.04

APPENDIX F:
Mean Values and Standard Deviations for Each Measure for Father-Present and Father-Absent Disadvantaged Children: Typical Groups Study

Measure	Black Females Father-Present (N=7) X̄	SD	Black Females Father-Absent (N=13) X̄	SD	Black Males Father-Present (N=8) X̄	SD	Black Males Father-Absent (N=12) X̄	SD	White Females Father-Present (N=9) X̄	SD	White Females Father-Absent (N=11) X̄	SD	White Males Father-Present (N=10) X̄	SD	White Males Father-Absent (N=10) X̄	SD
Verbal Creativity:																
Originality per response	2.07	37	2.34	51	3.19	73	2.72	75	2.84	75	2.64	49	3.00	40	2.74	67
Highest originality	3.14	88	3.62	92	4.91	86	3.36	1.15	3.78	1.06	3.89	69	4.22	54	3.48	86
Fluency	10.72	4 82	11.65	3.95	10.75	5.02	7.75	2.61	7.62	3.19	11.86	3.71	9.95	3.00	11.80	4.95
Flexibility	3.78	1 53	4.69	1.78	4.12	1.56	4.45	1.94	3.45	1.48	5.22	2.04	4.75	84	3.95	2.34
Dog and Bone:																
Quality per path	1.33	41	.94	42	1.26	40	1.22	43	.77	41	1.01	62	1.08	43	1.18	56
Highest quality	2.43	50	2.15	36	2.50	50	2.58	49	1.89	57	2.09	79	2.20	60	2.50	67
Token-in-the-Box:																
Quality per attempt	4.11	1 33	3.45	91	3.49	57	4.13	90	3.62	1.09	3.65	1.01	3.55	90	4.09	1.65
Highest quality	6.29	1 75	5.69	1.07	5.88	93	5.92	95	5.44	1.42	6.09	1.00	6.10	94	5.90	1.45
Five-Objects:																
Highest number	4.71	45	4.23	80	4.25	66	4.58	49	4.56	83	4.54	66	4.10	70	4.40	80
Reading:																
First attempt	1.00	0 00	1.46	75	1.38	70	1.67	74	1.11	31	1.00	0.00	1.40	49	1.20	40
Mean attempt	1.59	20	1.69	34	1.60	33	1.57	34	1.78	39	1.53	32	1.70	31	1.77	25
Risk	14.29	1 83	12.62	2.50	12.38	3.60	13.25	4.08	13.44	2.83	12.46	3.80	13.50	2.29	13.20	1.60
Balancing:																
First attempt	2.14	64	2.31	82	1.62	86	1.75	72	2.00	94	1.64	64	2.00	89	2.50	67
Mean attempt	1.90	15	1.90	28	1.83	19	1.82	26	1.83	34	1.76	23	1.88	21	2.07	20
Risk	13.14	2 59	12.31	2.40	14.25	2.95	14.08	1.94	13.44	3.24	13.64	2.96	13.80	1.99	14.30	2.90
Token-in-the-Box:																
Percent expecting success	85.71	—	76.92	—	100.00	—	91.67	—	66.67	—	100.00	—	100.00	—	100.00	—

(continued)

APPENDIX F: (continued)

Measure	Black Females Father-Present (N = 7) X̄	SD	Black Females Father-Absent (N = 13) X̄	SD	Black Males Father-Present (N = 8) X̄	SD	Black Males Father-Absent (N = 12) X̄	SD	White Females Father-Present (N = 9) X̄	SD	White Females Father-Absent (N = 11) X̄	SD	White Males Father-Present (N = 10) X̄	SD	White Males Father-Absent (N = 10) X̄	SD
Find-the-Surprise:																
Percent with autonomous first choice	42.86	—	53.86	—	62.50	—	58.33	—	88.89	—	72.73	—	70.00	—	80.00	—
Total autonomous responses	2.43	.90	2.08	1.38	2.38	1.41	2.25	1.23	3.44	.96	3.00	1.13	2.10	1.30	3.10	.94
Opening Doors:																
Number blank	6.86	3.23	6.38	4.14	7.62	3.71	8.33	4.44	9.56	2.99	6.45	6.23	8.80	5.08	8.30	3.55
Dog and Bone:																
Time to frustration	163.00	36.16	135.15	58.59	168.75	53.10	151.08	75.20	117.78	54.85	120.73	51.74	141.50	45.70	141.00	62.38
Token-in-the-Box:																
Number of attempts	21.29	6.56	15.92	6.37	19.00	7.78	17.50	7.34	26.44	11.43	24.27	6.12	19.50	5.78	19.00	7.56
Puzzle:																
Total time	180.00	0.00	169.62	18.34	169.25	21.14	180.00	0.00	180.00	0.00	180.00	0.00	180.00	0.00	177.20	7.76
Walk-the-Board:																
Handholding requests	13.86	6.68	13.08	6.32	7.62	8.00	4.58	7.75	15.00	6.07	14.18	5.83	6.50	8.04	10.00	7.00
Puzzle:																
Dependency statements per minute	.54	.48	.66	.48	.72	.60	.36	.60	.66	.54	.42	.36	.24	.30	.66	.60
Five-Objects:																
Requests for feedback	5.00	3.89	6.46	5.09	4.38	2.83	4.58	3.04	5.78	3.82	8.46	9.93	6.30	4.15	5.40	3.35
Percent needing prompting	14.29	—	0.00	—	12.50	—	8.33	—	0.00	—	0.00	—	0.00	—	10.00	—
Self-Concept:																
Total score	13.29	.70	13.92	1.44	13.50	.71	13.42	1.19	12.67	.67	13.91	1.68	12.90	.94	13.40	2.80
Teacher Thinks:																
Total score	13.29	.88	13.31	1.26	13.12	.60	13.25	1.48	13.11	1.52	13.00	1.04	12.90	1.76	13.30	2.00
Teacher Ratings:																
Total score	48.14	5.62	49.92	6.54	52.62	5.05	51.50	10.99	51.78	9.88	42.73	6.58	47.10	5.13	45.00	4.69

APPENDIX G:
Mean Values and Standard Deviations on Each Measure for Disadvantaged Black Children Who Attended Predominantly Black Versus Predominantly White Schools

Measure	Matched Groups Study				Typical Groups Study			
	Predominantly Black School (N = 19)		Predominantly White School (N = 29)		Predominantly Black School (N = 16)		Predominantly White School (N = 24)	
	$\bar{X}$	SD	$\bar{X}$	SD	$\bar{X}$	SD	$\bar{X}$	SD
Verbal Creativity:								
Quality per response	2.96	.84	2.70	.64	2.41	.83	2.69	.63
Highest originality	4.14	1.00	4.01	.86	3.52	1.30	4.12	.92
Fluency	10.71	3.98	9.70	4.62	9.69	5.13	10.44	3.68
Flexibility	4.10	1.13	4.17	1.68	3.41	1.79	4.98	1.47
Dog and Bone:								
Quality per path	1.11	.44	1.02	.56	1.07	.43	1.21	.44
Highest quality	2.32	.65	2.10	.71	2.38	.48	2.42	.49
Token-in-the-Box:								
Quality per attempt	3.81	1.20	3.58	.98	3.64	1.03	3.87	.96
Highest quality	5.68	1.66	5.62	1.58	5.56	1.37	6.12	.97
Five-Objects:								
Highest number	4.53	.82	4.48	.68	4.31	.77	4.50	.58
Reading:								
First attempt	1.32	.65	1.34	.71	1.38	.70	1.46	.71
Mean attempt	1.75	.33	1.50	.42	1.55	.37	1.67	.28
Risk	13.10	1.97	10.76	3.59	13.81	3.61	12.54	2.90
Balancing:								
First attempt	1.58	.75	1.76	.77	1.94	.90	2.00	.76
Mean attempt	1.86	.22	1.68	.25	1.77	.21	1.92	.24
Risk	14.53	2.62	12.69	2.88	12.88	2.96	13.71	2.21
Token-in-the-Box:								
Percent expecting success	73.7	—	65.5	—	93.7	—	83.3	—

(continued)

121

APPENDIX G: *(continued)*

Measure	Matched Groups Study				Typical Groups Study			
	Predominantly Black School (N = 19)		Predominantly White School (N = 29)		Predominantly Black School (N = 16)		Predominantly White School (N = 24)	
	$\bar{X}$	SD	$\bar{X}$	SD	$\bar{X}$	SD	$\bar{X}$	SD
Find-the-Surprise:								
Percent with autonomous first choice	47.4	—	55.2	—	56.2	—	54.2	—
Total autonomous responses	2.37	1.42	2.34	1.37	2.56	1.22	2.04	1.27
Opening Doors:								
Number blank	6.37	5.50	7.34	5.17	6.31	4.28	7.96	3.81
Dog and Bone:								
Time to frustration	135.42	35.13	134.14	67.24	139.50	59.11	159.54	61.64
Token-in-the-Box:								
Number of attempts	20.32	7.85	17.52	9.49	15.69	6.06	19.46	7.58
Puzzle:								
Total time	169.95	28.81	174.66	14.29	173.19	16.36	175.33	14.03
Walk-the-Board:								
Handholding requests	9.21	8.40	9.55	8.36	12.56	7.52	7.58	8.01
Puzzle:								
Dependency statements per minute	.42	.78	.48	.54	.72	.54	.42	.54
Five-Objects:								
Requests for feedback	7.47	7.02	4.38	2.58	5.00	4.40	5.38	3.75
Percent needing prompting	10.5	—	3.4	—	0.0	—	12.5	—
Self-Concept:								
Total score	13.58	1.23	13.34	1.15	13.69	.92	13.50	1.29
Teacher Thinks:								
Total score	13.10	1.21	13.10	1.16	13.00	.79	13.42	1.35
Teacher Ratings:								
Total score	49.26	7.90	50.07	9.10	51.25	5.96	50.21	9.00

APPENDIX H:
Correlations Among the Demographic and Standardized Test Measures (N = 304)

	Race (W/B)	Sex (F/M)	Father (Ab/Pr)	Study (M/T)	Bused (No/Yes)	School (% White)	Sibs (#)	Repeated a grade (No/Yes)	IQ	MA (in yrs.)	CA (in yrs.)	Reading Ach.	Arith. Ach.
SES (D/A)	.00	.00	.51**	.17**	.15**	.29**	-.04	-.26**	.34**	.22**	-.10	.31**	.29**
Race (W/B)		.00	-.07	.00	.24**	-.62**	-.16**	.06	-.26**	-.19**	.06	-.13*	-.13*
Sex (F/M)			.01	.00	.04	.06	-.00	.10	.08	.10	.07	-.05	.02
Father (Ab/Pr)				.01	.02	.19**	-.01	-.18*	.28**	.18**	-.10	.19**	.10
Study (M/T)					-.05	.00	-.04	.31**	.13*	.02	-.11	-.07	.01
Bused (No/Yes)						.06	-.13*	-.07	-.02	.03	.07	.10	.11
School (% White)							.00	-.18*	.29*	.23**	-.02	.22**	.23**
Sibs (#)								.19*	-.07	-.03	.04	-.07	-.04
Repeated a grade (no/Yes)[a]									-.22**	.08	.44**	-.01	-.02
IQ										.71**	-.24**	.34**	.30**
MA											.50**	.55**	.57**
CA												.32**	.43**
Reading Ach.													.69**

[a] The correlations between the variable "repeated grade" and other variables are based on N = 160 for the typical sample only.

*p < .05.

**p < .01.

APPENDIX I:
Correlations Between Demographic and Standardized Test Measures and the Children's Performance on the Experimental Measures
(N = 304)

	SES (D/A)	Race (W/B)	Sex (F/M)	Father (Ab/Pr)	Study (M/T)	Bused (No/Yes)	School (% White)	Sibs (#)	Repeated grade (No/Yes)[a]	IQ	MA	CA	Reading Ach.	Arith. Ach.
Verbal Creativity:														
Originality per response	.20***		.21***	.21***						.21***	.24***		.20***	.21***
Highest originality			.16**	.16**							.17**		.12*	.14*
Fluency	-.21***			-.19***			-.12*		.16*	-.14*			-.16**	
Flexibility	-.15**											.12*		
Dog and Bone:														
Quality per path	.12*				.12*					.18**	.24***		.15*	.23***
Highest quality	.12*											.12*	.12*	
Token-in-the-Box:														
Quality per attempt										.18**	.24***			
Highest quality												.14*		
Five-Objects:														
Highest number														
Reading:														
First attempt	.29***			.12*				-.14*		.26***	.27***		.35***	.31***
Mean attempt	.26***	-.15**		.14*			.11*			.34****	.31***		.51***	.37***
Risk					.16**		-.17***		-.14*					
Balancing:														
First attempt				-.13*										.14*
Mean attempt											.16**	.16**	.21***	.26***
Risk														
Token-in-the-Box:														
Expectancy of success														

	1	2	3	4	5	6	7	8	9
Find-the-Surprise:									
First choice				.14*		.16**	.21***	.14*	.16**
Total autonomous responses						.13*	.21***	.14*	.13*
Opening Doors:									
Number blank	.21***	−.15*		.20***		.18**	.22***	.26***	.22***
Dog and Bone:									
Time to frustration		.11*							
Token-in-the-Box:									
Number of attempts		−.12*				−.17**	.13*		
Puzzle:									
Total time	−.13*			.14*					
Walk-the-Board:									
Handholding requests		−.32**					−.19***		
Puzzle:									
Number of dependency statements	−.17**			−.19***	.17*	−.13*			
Five-Objects:									
Requests for feedback		.14*	−.13*						
Needed prompting	−.14*					.16**			.14*
Self-Concept:									
Total score								.16**	.14*
Teacher Thinks:									
Total score							.13*		
Teacher Ratings:									
Total score	.21***	.14*		.18**		.25***	.17**	.45***	.30***

ªThe correlations between the variable "repeated grade" and other variables are based on $N = 160$ for the typical sample only.

$*p < .05$

$**p < .01$

$***p < .001$

References

Achenbach, T., & Zigler, E. Social competence and self-image disparity in psychiatric and nonpsychiatric patients. *Journal of Abnormal and Social Psychology*, 1963, *67*(3), 197–205.

Alper, T. G., Blane, H. T., & Abrams, B. K. Reactions of middle and lower class children to finger paints as a function of class differences in child-training practices. *Journal of Abnormal and Social Psychology*, 1955, *51*, 439–448.

Banta, T. J. *Tests for the evaluation of early childhood education: The Cincinnati Autonomy Test Battery*. Unpublished manuscipt, University of Cincinnati, 1967.

Baratz, S. B., & Baratz, J. C. Early childhood intervention: The social science base of instructional racism. *Harvard Educational Review*, 1970, *40*, 29–50.

Bateson, G. *Steps to an ecology of mind: Collected essays in anthropology, psychiatry, evolution and epistemology*. San Francisco: Chandler, 1972.

Berstein, B. Social class and linguistic development: A theory of social learning. In A. H. Halsey, J. Floud, & C. A. Anderson (Eds.), *Education, economy and society*. Glencoe, Ill.: Free Press, 1961.

Blurton Jones, N. G., & Konner, M. J. !Kung knowledge of animal behavior. In R. Lee & I. DeVore (Eds.), *Kalahari hunter–gatherers*. Cambridge, Mass.: Harvard University Press, 1976.

Bronfenbrenner, U. *Who cares for America's children?* Unpublished manuscript, Cornell University, 1975.

Brown, B. *The assessment of self-concept among 4-year-old Negro and white children: A comparative study using the Brown IDS Self-concept Referrents Test*. New York: Institute for Developmental Studies, New York Medical College, 1966.

Brownfain, J. J. Stability of the self-concept as a dimension of personality. *Journal of Abnormal and Social Psychology*, 1952, *47*, 597–606.

Caldwell, B. M. The effects of infant care. In M. L. Hoffman & L. W. Hoffman (Eds.), *Review of child development research* (Vol. 1). New York: Russell Sage Foundation, 1964.

Campbell, D. T., & Erlebacher, A. How regression artifacts in quasi-experimental evaluations can mistakenly make compensatory education look harmful. In J.

Hellmuth (Ed.), *Compensatory education: A national debate.* Vol. III of *The disadvantaged child.* New York: Brunner/Mazel, 1970.

Campbell, D. T., & Stanley, J. C. *Experimental and quasi-experimental designs for research.* Chicago: Rand McNally, 1966.

Chen, M. K. A critical look at the matching technique in experimentation. *Journal of Experimental Education,* 1967, *35*(4), 95–98.

Coates, B. White adult behavior toward black and white children. *Child Development,* 1972, *43*, 143–154.

Cole, M., & Brunner, J. S. Cultural differences and inferences about psychological processes. *American Psychologist,* 1971, *26*, 867–876.

Cole, M., Gay, J., Glick, J., & Sharp, D. *The cultural context of learning and thinking.* New York: Basic Books, 1971.

Crandall, V. C. Personality characteristics and social and achievement behaviors associated with children's social desirability response tendencies. *Journal of Personality and Social Psychology,* 1966, *4*, 477–486.

Cronbach, L. J., & Meehl, P. E. Construct validity in psychological tests. *Psychological Bulletin,* 1955, *52*, 281–302.

Crowne, D., & Marlowe, D. *The approval motive: Studies in evaluative dependence.* New York: Wiley, 1964.

Deutsch, C. Social class and child development. In B. M. Caldwell & H. Ricciuti (Eds.), *Review of child development research* (Vol. 3). Chicago: University of Chicago Press, 1973.

Deutsch, M., Katz, I., & Jensen, A. R. *Social class, race, and psychological development.* New York: Holt, Rinehart & Winston, 1968.

Dobzhansky, T. *Genetic diversity and human equality.* New York: Basic Books, 1973.

Dreger, R. M., & Miller, K. S. Comparative psychological studies of Negroes and Whites in the United States. *Psychological Bulletin,* 1960, *57*, 361–402.

Dreger, R. M., & Miller, K. S. Comparative psychological studies of Negroes and Whites in the United States: 1959–1965. *Psychological Bulletin,* 1968, *70*, 1–58.

Garner, W. R., Hake, H. W., & Eriksen, C. W. Operationism and the concept of perception. *Psychological Review,* 1956, *63*, 149–159.

Gewirtz, J. Three determinants of attention-seeking in young children. *Monographs of the Society for Research in Child Development,* 1954, *19*(2, Serial No. 59).

Goss, A. M. Estimated versus actual physical strength in three ethnic groups. *Child Development,* 1968, *39*, 283–290.

Gottesman, I. I. Personality and natural selection. In S. G. Vandenberg (Ed.), *Methods and goals in human behavior genetics.* New York: Academic Press, 1965.

Guilford, J. P. The structure of intellect. *Psychological Bulletin,* 1956, *53*, 267–293.

Guilford, J. P., Wilson, R. C., Christensen, P. R., & Lewis, D. J. A factor-analytic study of creative thinking: I. Hypotheses and description of tests. *Reports from the Psychological Laboratory* (No. 3). Los Angeles: University of Southern California, 1951.

Harter, S., & Zigler, E. The assessment of effectance motivation in normal and retarded children. *Developmental Psychology,* 1974, *10*, 169–180.

Heathers, G. Emotional dependence and independence in a physical threat situation. *Child Development,* 1953, *24*, 169–179.

Herrnstein, R. J. *I.Q. in the meritocracy.* Boston: Little, Brown, 1973.

Hersch, C. The cognitive functioning of the creative person: A developmental analysis. *Journal of Projective Techniques,* 1962, *26*, 193–200.

Hertzig, M. E., Birch, H., Thomas, A., & Mendez, O. A. Class and ethnic differences in the responsiveness of preschool children to cognitive demands. *Monographs of the Society for Research in Child Development*, 1968, *33*(1, Serial No. 117).

Herzog, E., & Sudia, C. Children in fatherless families. In B. M. Caldwell & H. Ricciuti (Eds.), *Review of child development research* (Vol. 3). Chicago: University of Chicago Press, 1973.

Hess, R. D. Social class and ethnic influences on socialization. In P. H. Mussen (Ed.), *Carmichael's manual of child psychology* (3rd ed.) (Vol. 2). New York: Wiley, 1970.

Hess, R. D., & Shipman, V. C. Cognitive elements in maternal behavior. In J. P. Hill (Ed.), *Minnesota Symposia on Child Psychology* (Vol. 1). Minneapolis: University of Minnesota Press, 1967.

Hillson, H. T., & Meyers, F. C. *The demonstration guidance project: 1957–1962.* New York: New York City Board of Education, 1963.

Hollingshead, A. B., & Redlich, F. C. *Social class and mental illness: A community study.* New York: Wiley, 1958.

Holt, J. *How children fail.* New York: Dell, 1964.

Hunt, J. McV. The psychological basis for using pre-school enrichment as an antidote for cultural deprivation. *Merrill-Palmer Quarterly*, 1964, *10*, 209–248.

Iscoe, I., & Pierce-Jones, J. Divergent thinking, age, and intelligence in White and Negro children. *Child Development*, 1964, *35*, 785–797.

Jacklin, C. M. & Mischel, H. N. As the twig is bent—sex role stereotyping in early readers. *School Psychology Digest*, 1973, *2*, 283–290.

Jacobson, L. I., Berger, S. E., Bergman, R. L., Millham, J., & Greeson, L. E. Effects of age, sex, systematic conceptual learning, acquisition of learning sets, and programmed social interaction on the intellectual and conceptual development of preschool children from poverty backgrounds. *Child Development*, 1971, *42*, 1399–1415.

Jencks, C., Smith, M., Acland, H., Bane, M. J., Cohen, D., Gintis, H., Heyns, B., & Michaelson, S. *Inequality: A reassessment of the effect of family and schooling in America.* New York: Basic Books, 1972.

Jensen, A. R. A theory of primary and secondary familial mental retardation. In N. R. Ellis (Ed.), *International review of research in mental retardation* (Vol. 4). New York: Academic Press, 1970.

Kardiner, A., & Ovesey, L. *The mark of oppression.* Cleveland, Ohio: World, 1951.

Katz, P. A., & Zigler, E. Self-image disparity: A developmental approach. *Journal of Personality and Social Psychology*, 1967, *5*, 186–195.

Kreitler, S., Zigler, E., & Kreitler, H. The nature of curiosity in children. *Journal of School Psychology*, 1975, *13*(3), 185–200.

Labov, W. The logic of nonstandard English. In F. Williams (Ed.), *Language and poverty*. Chicago: Markham Publ. Co., 1970.

Lamb, M. E. The role of the father: An overview. In M. E. Lamb (Ed.), *The role of the father in child development*. New York: Wiley, 1976.

Lesser, G. S., Fifer, G., & Clark, D. H. Mental abilities of children in different social class and cultural groups. *Monographs of the Society for Research in Child Development*, 1965, *30*(4, Serial No. 102).

Loehlin, J. C., Lindzey, G., & Spuhler, J. N. *Race differences in intelligence.* San Francisco: Freeman, 1975.

Maccoby, E., & Jacklin, C. *The psychology of sex differences.* Stanford, Calif.: Stanford University Press, 1974.

McDermott, R. P., & Aron, J. Pirandello in the classroom: On the possibility of equal educational opportunity in American culture. In M. C. Reynolds (Ed.), *Futures of education for exceptional students: Emerging structures.* Minneapolis: National Support Systems Project, University of Minnesota, 1978.

Meehl, P. E. Nuisance variables and the ex post facto design. In M. Radner & S. Winokur (Eds.), *Minnesota studies in the philosophy of science* (Vol. 4). Minneapolis: University of Minnesota Press, 1970.

Meehl, P. E. High school yearbooks: A reply to Schwartz. *Journal of Abnormal Psychology,* 1971, *77*(2), 143–148.

Messer, S. B. Reflection–impulsivity: A review. *Psychological Bulletin,* 1976, *83*(6), 1026–1052.

Mosteller, F., & Moynihan, D. P. (Eds.). *On equality of educational opportunity.* New York: Random House, 1972.

Nobles, W. W. Psychological research and the Black self-concept: A critical review. *Journal of Science Issues,* 1973, *29*(1), 11–31.

Pasamanick, B., & Knobloch, H. Epidemiologic studies on the complications of pregnancy and the birth process. In G. Caplan (Ed.), *Prevention of mental disorders in childhood.* New York: Basic Books, 1961.

Pettigrew, T. F. *A profile of the Negro American.* Princeton, N.J.: Van Nostrand, 1964.

Rist, R. *The urban school.* Cambridge, Mass.: MIT Press, 1973.

Rogers, D. Visual expression: Creative advantage of the disadvantaged. *The Elementary School Journal,* 1968(May), 395–399.

Rosenberg, M., & Simmons, R. G. *Black and white self-esteem: The urban school child* (M. Arnold & C. Rose, Monograph Series). Washington, D.C.: American Sociological Association, 1971.

Rosenthal, R., & Jacobson, L. *Pygmalion in the classroom.* New York: Holt, Rinehart & Winston, 1968.

Rubovits, P. C., & Maehr, M. L. Pygmalion black and white. *Journal of Personality and Social Psychology,* 1973, *25*(2), 210–218.

St. John, N. H. *School desegregation: Outcomes for children.* New York: Wiley, 1975.

St. John, N. H., & Smith, M. S. *School racial composition, achievement, and aspiration.* Unpublished manuscript, Harvard University Graduate School of Education, 1969.

Sattler, J. Racial "experimenter effects" in experimentation, testing, interviewing, and psychotherapy. *Psychological Bulletin,* 1970, *73,* 137–160.

Scribner, S., & Cole, M. Cognitive consequences of formal and informal education. *Science,* 1973, *182,* 553–559.

Seitz, V. *Long-term motivational-cognitive effects of day care* (Final report for Grant No. OCD-CB-292). Washington, D.C.: Office of Child Development, 1974.

Seitz, V., Abelson, W., Levine, E., & Zigler, E. Effects of place of testing on the Peabody Picture Vocabulary Test scores of disadvantaged Head Start and non-Head Start children. *Child Development,* 1975, *46*(2), 481–486.

Silverstein, B., & Krate, R. *Children of the dark ghetto: A developmental psychology.* New York: Praeger, 1975.

Soares, A. T., & Soares, L. M. Self-perceptions of culturally disadvantaged children. *American Educational Research Journal,* 1969, *6,* 31–45.

Stein, A. Strategies for failure. *Harvard Educational Review,* 1971, *41*(2), 158–204.

Stodolosky, S., & Lesser, G. Learning patterns in the disadvantaged. *Harvard Educational Review,* 1967, *37*(4), 546–593.

Thomas, A., Hertzig, M. E., Dryman, I., & Fernandez, P. Examiner effect in IQ testing of Puerto Rican working-class children. *American Journal of Orthopsychiatry*, 1971, *41*, 809–821.

Torrance, P. E. *Rewarding creative behavior: Experiments in classroom creativity.* Englewood Cliffs, N.J.: Prentice-Hall, 1965.

Trowbridge, N. Self-concept and socio-economic status in elementary school children. *American Educational Research Journal*, 1972, *9*, 525–537.

Tulkin, S. R., & Konner, M. J. Alternative conceptions of intellectual functioning. *Human Development*, 1973, *16*, 33–52.

Tyler, S. *Cognitive anthropology.* New York: Holt, Rinehart & Winston, 1970.

Veroff, J., & Peele, S. Initial effects of desegregation on the achievement motivation of Negro elementary school children. *Journal of Social Issues*, 1969, *25*(3), 77–91.

Wallach, M. A., & Kogan, N. *Modes of thinking in young children: A study of the creativity–intelligence distinction.* New York: Holt, Rinehart & Winston, 1965.

Ward, W. C. Creativity in young children. *Child Development*, 1968, *39*, 737–754.

Wilson, A. B. Social stratification and academic achievement. In A. H. Passow (Ed.), *Education in depressed areas.* New York: Bureau of Publications, Teachers College, Columbia University, 1963.

Winer, B. J. *Statistical principles in experimental design* (2nd ed.). New York: McGraw-Hill, 1971.

Yamamoto, K. *Experimental scoring manual for the Minnesota Tests of Creative Thinking.* Kent, Ohio: Bureau of Educational Research, Kent State University, 1964.

Yamamoto, K., & Chimbidis, M. E. Achievement, intelligence and creative thinking in fifth-grade children: A correlational study. *Merrill-Palmer Quarterly*, 1966, *12*, 233–241.

Yando, R., Zigler, E., & Gates, M. The influence of Negro and White teachers rated as effective or noneffective on the performance of Negro and White lower-class children. *Developmental Psychology*, 1971, *5*(2), 290–299.

Zigler, E. The environmental mystique: Training the intellect versus development of the child. *Childhood Education*, 1970, *46*, 402–412.

Zigler, E. Project Head Start: Success or failure? *Learning*, 1973, *1*, 43–47.

Zigler, E., Abelson, W. D., & Seitz, V. Motivational factors in the performance of economically disadvantaged children on the Peabody Picture Vocabulary Test. *Child Development*, 1973, *44*, 294–303.

Zigler, E., & Butterfield, E. C. Motivational aspects of changes in I.Q. test performance of culturally deprived nursery school children. *Child Development*, 1968, *39*(1), 1–14.

Zigler, E., & Child, I. L. (Eds.) *Socialization and personality development.* Reading, Mass.: Addison-Wesley, 1973.

Author Index

Subject Index